WHERE DID
NOAH
PARK THE ARK?

WHERE DID NOAH PARK THE ARK?

ANCIENT MEMORY TECHNIQUES FOR REMEMBERING PRACTICALLY ANYTHING

ERAN KATZ

THREE RIVERS PRESS · NEW YORK

Library of Congress Cataloging-in-Publication Data is available upon
request.

ISBN 978-0-307-59197-5

Printed in the United States of America

Design by Cynthia Dunne

10 9 8 7 6 5 4 3 2 1

First Edition

For my loving family and friends. You have helped me find my passion in life. I just can't remember what it is. . . .

CONTENTS

Contents

PREFACE

MY DAUGHTER GALI was four years old when she surprised me one evening as we walked down the pedestrian mall in the center of Jerusalem together.

"Daddy, can I have a coin?" she asked.

"What for?" I inquired.

"To give to Boris," she replied.

I didn't know a Boris, especially one who conducted business with my young daughter. So I asked her, "Who exactly is Boris?"

"Come on, you know," she said in a small voice. "The man who plays music."

I realized that she was referring to the street musician who plays the mandolin and relies on the charity and kindness of passersby for his living. Nevertheless, I was surprised by the fact that she knew his name.

Gali took a coin from me and approached the musician. She stood in front of him and, in a quiet voice, said, "Boris, this is for you."

The musician looked up with astonishment. "How do you know that my name is Boris?" he asked with a heavy Russian accent.

My daughter looked at him for a moment and said, "You told me last time!"

"But how did you remember?" he asked, his eyes twinkling.

My daughter couldn't answer him. It was as if she were thinking, "What's the problem? You told me your name and I remembered it. Why the big surprise?"

I observed the two of them in amazement. I recalled hearing his name before, but I had completely forgotten it. For me he was just an ordinary person, the type one passes by with hardly a blink of the eye. But for Gali, he was *Boris!* Not only a man with a name, but one who makes her happy through his music.

Boris straightened up, picked up the mandolin, and began strumming a tune. Gali placed a coin inside the rusty tin can and, at that moment, Boris stopped playing. He knelt, took the coin out of the tin, and returned it to Gali.

"You are my friend," he said with a warmhearted smile. "I'll play for you for nothing."

I have been developing and applying memory techniques for years, aware of the potency and importance of a sound memory. But what transpired that day was an absolute revelation—a four-year-old girl approached a street musician and addressed him by name. The musician, whose livelihood depends on every cent dropped into his tin can, refused the money. Why? Because one person among the throngs of people who pass by him every day remembered his name!

That's all that Gali did. Boris, touched to the core, thanked her in the most natural but amazing manner—he dedicated a song to her for free. In his way, he thanked her for remembering his most dear possession—his name.

A good memory is a valuable asset. It is the most important tool we possess. Yet how little we invest in it, train it, and nurture it.

During the ancient Greek and Roman eras, great emphasis was placed on developing memory skills. Plato, Aristotle, and other educators obsessively sought to understand the human memory and improve man's memory abilities.

I was introduced to their methods about twenty-four years ago, while reading Harry Lorayne's memory books. As the years passed, I turned a casual interest in memory into an exceptional hobby: I learned to perform extraordinary memory stunts, refined their methods, invented new ones of my own, and discovered their efficiency in every area of life.

In this book, I will introduce you to what, in my opinion, are the most successful ideas, methods, and tricks available to develop an excellent memory. Many of the methods you'll find are based on ancient wisdom, mainly from Jewish experience.

Why Jewish?

Well, the Jewish answer to that would be "Why not?"

Actually, there's much to learn from the Jewish experience, especially when it comes to memory. Jews struggled throughout the ages to maintain their tradition under extreme hardship, and in order to achieve this goal, they developed advanced memory techniques from which each and every one of us can benefit. My fluency in Hebrew has afforded me the opportunity to delve into rare, original holy texts that discuss ancient methods for remembering facts, figures, and stories. The majority of these texts are unknown to the general public and privately owned by Jewish friends of mine and scholars. Some of the techniques were adopted by the ancient Greeks and Romans; many are being revealed for the first time in this memory improvement book.

In addition, I've embraced the Talmudic saying "I have learned much from my teachers, but more from my colleagues, and most of all from my pupils." That's why I will share with you the valuable insights and suggestions I collected from students who participated in my workshops, implemented these techniques, and provided priceless feedback and new ideas. A valuable combination of the best of old methods and cutting-edge new techniques, this book will show you how to remember information quickly, efficiently, and—most important—correctly.

Throughout the book I'll challenge you with amusing yet practical exercises, building the level of difficulty as we go along. I promise you will notice a change in your ability to remember details once you have read the first few chapters of the book.

After finishing this book, you will be able to perform extraordinary memory exercises and, for the rest of your life, carry the knowledge, experience, and proof that your memory is trustworthy and capable of performing for the long haul.

PART I

BREAKING
THE ICE

WHY DON'T YOU
MINGLE A BIT WITH
YOUR MEMORY.
IT'S ABOUT TIME YOU
TWO GET ACQUAINTED.

~~~~~~~~~~~~~~~~~~

CHAPTER 1

THE BIG LIE

(Not *That* Big Lie . . . Just Some Surprising Ones About Our Memory)

YOU'RE STROLLING THROUGH the mall, swarms of people passing you by, when suddenly he appears.

His face looks incredibly familiar, and his name is at the tip of your tongue. A phony grin is plastered across your face. You're optimistic that as he nears, you'll magically recall his name. But as he extends his hand, you withdraw in defeat.

"Please remind me," you say apologetically.

"At the Schmendrikson bar mitzvah two months ago. You're Michael, right?"

"Wow! Well done," you blurt out. "And you're Ron—um, John. I mean Sean."

"Nathan," he puts in quickly.

"Right! I remembered something with an *N*." Sweat

beads form across your brow. "Forgive me, I have a terrible memory."

Sound familiar? Let's continue.

You return home for a change of clothes before heading out to the gym. You're all set to go, clad in your sweatsuit, the Howard Johnson's towel neatly tucked in your bag, and your keys . . . your keys . . . where are your keys?

You rummage through your briefcase, go to the kitchen table, and from there move to the coffee table in the living room. You stop and think for a moment—no, they've got to be in your briefcase.

This time you empty out your briefcase. Not there—you put everything back in. So maybe they're in the laptop bag—that must be it! You tear through the bag as if you're a hungry dog on the scent of a T-bone. Still no keys.

You take a deep breath and think.

What was I doing? Came in the door, went to the bathroom, then into the kitchen . . .

They *must* be in the briefcase. You again dump out its contents, this time with greater fervor, and jab your fingertips into every little nook and cranny. *Still* no keys. With temples throbbing, you call the friend that you were supposed to pick up ten minutes ago.

"I can't find my keys. I've lost my mind."

Then suddenly, next to the phone, you notice that your phone book is awkwardly propped up—by the keys.

Relief washes over you and you bolt out the door.

"What should I conclude?" you may ask. "That my memory is failing me? I know! That's why I'm reading this book."

No, that's not it. The common mistake most of us make is that we *decide* we have a bad memory.

SURPRISE #1: THERE'S NO SUCH THING
AS A BAD MEMORY

There's a misconception that falls into one of two camps: either you have a good memory or you have a bad one. If you have difficulty remembering Sarah's phone number, this doesn't indicate that you have a bad memory in general. All it means is that you have difficulty remembering Sarah's phone number. Perhaps you should try Dinah's. She's a nice girl. Good family. Her father is a wealthy physician.

If you've forgotten most of what you've learned while cramming for the bar exam, does it mean that you're developing acute Alzheimer's? No! You may simply be under a lot of pressure. Or you've been studying law to satisfy your mother, who doesn't appreciate the fact that you're one of the greatest saxophone players since William Jefferson Clinton, and has no faith in your ability to make a living as such. What kind of profession is a saxophonist? Look at the Meltzers—all three sons are lawyers.

> "I know only two tunes. One is 'Yankee Doodle' and the other isn't."
> —GENERAL ULYSSES S. GRANT

Your memory may be weak when it comes to recalling phone numbers and legal cases, but you easily remember the lyrics to a song you've heard just a few times.

It's feasible to have a good memory for certain information and a poor memory for other data. For most of us, that's the case. The minute you realize it's not all or nothing, your task becomes easier—you need improvement only in the weaker areas of your memory.

SURPRISE #2: YOUR MEMORY IS BETTER THAN YOU THINK

"Give me a break!" you're probably thinking. "If I don't remember where I placed my keys, and three times a week it takes me half an hour to find them, then for goodness' sake, my memory is not only bad, it's nonexistent!"

You're being too hard on yourself, I promise. In reality, we simply underestimate our memory.

Benjamin Disraeli, former British prime minister, once said that there are three kinds of lies—good lies, evil lies, and statistics. Let's talk about the statistics kind of lie.

How many times in the last month has it taken you more than ten minutes to find your keys? Three? Four? Ten?

Statistically, we use our keys 150 times a month. Locking up the house, driving, opening the mailbox, uncuffing Uncle Harold. Let's say that you couldn't find your keys ten times in one month, which seems like a big memory loss problem. But look at it this way—140 times you *did* know where they were. That's a 95 percent success rate!

Our sense of memory failure is totally disproportional.

If your "no-good, lousy, incompetent" memory fails only 5 percent of the time, don't you wish that you could have a 5 percent failure ratio in everything you do in life?

Why are so many of us convinced that we suffer from memory problems? Simply put, a small failure often casts a shadow on a long line of successes.

If we receive all A's on a report card with the exception of a C in one course, we feel a twinge of failure. We may get great feedback following a presentation we delivered, but if one participant comes over to us afterward and says, "By the way, remember you mentioned the rapper 50 Bucks? Well, it's 50 Cent," we'll free-fall from our self-esteem summit.

We're emotional perfectionists with an inclination toward exaggeration. That is why we spotlight the meager 5 percent of the time we didn't find our keys rather than the 95 percent of the time we did. (Though we did eventually find them, didn't we? It's just that our memory didn't work at XP speed.)

The same statistics usually apply in other memory-related areas.

As in the case of the keys, every month you run into lots of people whose names you *do* remember. But if within a month you run into five people you don't remember, you jump to the conclusion that your ability to remember names is deficient.

In addition, by expecting that you will always remember someone's name the moment you see her, you've set yourself up for failure. And then you make your big mistake—you apologize. You apologize once, you apologize twice, and slowly you develop the inner belief that you have a bad memory for people's names.

Next time you won't even bother trying to remember someone's name, an appointment, or a task, because you've already accepted that it's a waste of time. This self-defeating process then often leads to making excuses when you've forgotten something: "I'm getting over a bad head cold," "I didn't get enough sleep this week," or "I have so much on my mind lately." (Which is like saying "My brain is very small, and if I had to remember the appointment with you, it would be at the expense of Debra's phone number, and I wanted to ask her out tonight.")

As a memory trainer, I've heard a vast array of excuses and complaints that could easily fill another book, which

I'd title *The "Excuse My Memory" Manual for Successful Incompetence*.

However, the one I would definitely rank as the number one best excuse I ever heard was at an international book fair I attended several years ago.

I was standing in my publisher's booth when a thin middle-aged man approached me.

"You're the memory guy, right?" he asked in a menacing tone, pointing at my chest.

"Eran Katz. Nice to meet you." I extended a hand shakily.

He looked me up and down, then said, "I bought your memory improvement book several months ago and it didn't help me."

There was an awkward moment of silence. His accusation drew attention, and some people glanced toward us.

"Which part of the book was difficult?" I asked, trying to swallow my pride. "Were there any specific techniques you had a hard time with?"

He looked at me with a dumbfounded expression.

"I don't know," he said, blinking nervously. "I haven't read the book yet."

Well, some problems can be solved fairly easily.

SURPRISE #3: AGE IS JUST AN EXCUSE

There's a proven correlation between age and memory, right?

Memory can deteriorate due to age-related physiological factors, resulting in a potentially debilitating medical condition, but for the majority of us age is an excuse. When we come home from work and discover that the report we intended to read before bed is still at the office, we shrug and say, "Age takes its toll."

I challenge you to a simple experiment. Walk over to any

elementary school of your choice at the end of the school day. Go into any classroom and see for yourself that poor memory isn't age-related. In *all* the classrooms you'll find bags, books, notebooks, coats, and an assortment of other items that were forgotten. The only difference between a seven-year-old who forgets to bring his lunch box home from school and a forty-five-year-old human resources manager who forgets to bring his report home from the office is that the kid doesn't come home and say helplessly: "Well, Mom, what can I do? My memory isn't what it used to be."

You shouldn't use the self-defeating excuse that because of your age, your memory is slipping away faster than certain men can unbutton a blouse. As long as you fine-tune your memory, trust it, and count on it, it will prove to be a worthy companion.

SURPRISE #4: YOUR MEMORY HAS NO LIMIT

Once when I was a university student, I arrived at the exam hall and greeted my friends with "Hey, what's up? How are things going?"

"Don't talk to me right now!" one of them shouted in panic. "I have exactly the amount of information I'll need for the exam in my head, and if you say something, it will enter one ear and part of what I need to know for the exam will exit the other!"

No, it won't.

It's not as if we have 5 gigabytes of memory capacity in our brain and that's all. The human mind can effortlessly absorb an incredible amount of information. Every day, unaware, we remember hundreds of thousands of information units—new things we've learned, news we've heard on the radio, conversations we've had with others, sights we've seen, sounds we've heard, every emotion, idea, and feeling we've experienced. Everything is registered and integrated into our memory.

We're even capable of writing about things we've memorized but have never even seen, such as dinosaurs, nuclear weapons, and what our teenage son's room looks like during the weekend.

Here's a shocking bit of news: the billions of things we will remember in our entire lifetime will take up a mere 10 percent of our memory capacity. Over 90 percent isn't even used. (With some people that's more evident than with others.) Do you really believe that a one-time shopping list will cause undue stress on your memory? Such a list won't even tickle your memory. Later on in this book you'll learn how to effortlessly remember a list faster than it would take you to write it down on a piece of paper. And I'll prove to you that you won't forget it even a few days after you've gone shopping.

Our inability to trust our memory isn't related only to new details we'd like to remember. The same applies to our existing memory bank as well. For example, think for a moment about the yield sign we encounter prior to turning at an intersection. What shape is the sign? Is it a regular triangle or is it inverted?

Think hard. Is it really inverted or does it just seem that way to you?

What if I tell you it's a regular triangle—are you surprised?

I won't keep you in suspense. It's an inverted triangle. But admit it—a smidgen of doubt crossed your mind.

The point is that it's easy to undermine our faith in our memory, because we don't truly trust it. Furthermore, we tend to rely on someone else's memory rather than on our own.

It's easier to believe three friends who claim that they

remember Roger Moore playing the part of James Bond in the movie *Never Say Never Again* even though we remember it was Sean Connery (it actually was Sean Connery).

There's a Yiddish saying—"If you don't believe in God, don't come with your complaints to Him." In other words, if you don't have faith in your memory, if you don't think this book can really help you, it won't. Refrain from excuses such as "I have a terrible memory," "My memory isn't what it used to be," or "I was born in Jimi Hendrix's trailer during Woodstock."

Now let's take this to the next level and learn how to develop such faith together.

CHAPTER 2

A NEW APPROACH

STEP 1: MOTIVATION FOR THE UNMOTIVATED

What is your motivation to remember something?

Motivation is a basic requirement for achieving anything in life, including a good memory.

You don't hear much about people forgetting to go to an important job interview, do you? And if someone is owed say, $100,000, odds are they're not going to forget about it. When motivated, people naturally remember.

As I mentioned in the preface, my interest in Jewish wisdom led me to fascinating memory techniques and principles to boost memory. So let's begin with the ultimate motivator, the one bestowed upon the people of Israel:

> *Remember what Amalek did to thee.*
> *Remember the Sabbath and to keep it holy.*
> *Remember these, O Yaakov, and Israel; thou*
>   *art my servant.*
> *Remember the days of old.*

Jews are the only people in the world with a religious commandment obligating them to remember. Talk about motivation—can you think of a greater incentive to a religious person than a direct commandment from God?

Even when writing became prevalent, Jewish sages preferred to transmit information orally. Jews in the Middle Ages didn't have any interest in writing down their history the way other cultures did. Had you been alive in the year A.D. 1500 and wanted to read about Jewish history, you would have had five books at your disposal. That was the entire written history from all previous generations in circulation, Torah (Old Testament) aside.

This may seem strange for anyone living in the twenty-first century who thinks that there is no substitute for pen and paper or a computer, but Jews have always believed that putting things down on paper doesn't necessarily help one remember. In fact, Jews have felt that writing things down permits one *not* to need to remember.

The truth is that more than once in their history, Jews' written records have been destroyed by rival cultures. Consequently, the Jewish people feared depending on physical property, such as books, to protect their history and traditions. In order to safeguard these precious parts of their culture, they had to depend on the one thing no one would be able to destroy: the collective memory of the Jewish people. While other societies were writing down their stories and histories, the Jews were motivated to develop their memory.

> "My teacher said I don't have motivation for anything . . . but I don't really feel like talking about this right now."
> —RODNEY DANGERFIELD

When I was a college student, I made a living tutoring

people in memory improvement. Once I was asked to the house of an elderly woman who wished to hire me. For an hour and a half, I made every effort to teach her how to easily recall locking the door upon leaving the house, take medications on time, and schedule appointments with doctors.

A week later, as I was walking down the street, I saw her and greeted her.

"Do we know each other?" she asked, confused. Obviously she didn't remember me.

This could be either a funny story or a sad one, depending on how you look at it.

Perhaps I should add that I didn't do much talking during that lesson. For every sentence I said, she replied with seven of her own, mainly about her childhood: how she'd fought the Germans during World War II, how she'd fought the Germans during World War I, how she'd fought the Germans during the French Revolution . . . She then went on to talk about her late husband and all the arguments and fights they had had. He was also German.

I am telling you about this for a reason, really. You cannot set a goal and achieve it if you don't truly want to, no matter how wonderful the tricks I'll teach you. That lady didn't want to learn how to improve her memory. She was simply lonely and wanted me to keep her company.

Is the purpose of this book to keep you company? Are you reading this book in bed right now hoping it will improve your memory *and* lull you to sleep? Allow me to recommend the annual federal budget report. It will do a better job.

It's normal to believe there's no way we can improve our memory. These doubts build each time our memory fails us, each time we forget someone's name or an important meeting we had scheduled. The accumulation of these "failures" gradually leads us to lose all motivation for improving our memory.

STEP 2: MOTIVATION FOR BEGINNERS

How can we motivate ourselves under such circumstances? By finding positive anchors. Remember the sweet moments of success in your life, when you were the one who got the job out of dozens of applicants, got an A on a tough exam, or signed a contract with a major publishing house? Those

> "Yes we can."
> —BARACK OBAMA

victories are similar to the pitons a mountain climber hammers into a crack in the rock, giving him the security, ability, and desire to keep climbing. They grant us the positive feedback we need, proving that it's possible to succeed and progress. By focusing on the times we do get it right, we garner the motivation crucial to flourish on the bumpy road of life.

It's the same with our memory. We have discussed the cases when you apologize to people whose names you forgot, and the sense of failure you feel when they remembered yours. But what about cases in reverse? Think about the time you *did* remember someone and he didn't remember you.

"Where do we know each other from?" he asks hesitantly.

You, experiencing the thrill of victory like a contestant on some game show who already knows the answer, confidently reply: "We met at the ski lodge at Killington last winter. You're Nathan, right?"

"Way to go," he says, impressed. "What a great memory."

Imagine a similar scenario happening to you the next day with someone else, and then again a week later, and each time you're complimented on your excellent memory. Naturally your confidence for remembering names will increase—along with your motivation to remember the name of a new person you meet in the future.

Think about Pavlov's famous experiment in which he conditioned a dog to salivate every time it heard a bell ring—a sure sign that food was on its way. Our brain is also conditioned. If we receive accolades for our keen ability to remember Top 40 music tunes, then our brain will make an extra effort every time we hear a new song on the radio. In essence, it will send us a message: "Listen carefully to the music and lyrics, and remember the band that is performing it, because you have an excellent memory for it."

On the other hand, if we develop a negative attitude toward our ability to remember birthdays, our brain will be programmed *not* to make any effort in even trying. "Next Thursday is my birthday," a colleague tells us joyfully, and our brain remains frozen in place, as if saying: "Drop it, don't bother—you won't remember this anyway since your memory for this area really sucks. Let's go get some ice cream or something."

You have to strive to preserve your memory's strengths, and change your attitude about what you consider its weaknesses. The next time you run into Allan and can't remember his name, don't apologize! Simply assure him that the next time you see him, you'll remember his name. And you will, because you've now planted a memory seed. In Chapter 19, you'll learn all about this trick for remembering names.

From now on, when it takes you fifteen minutes to find your keys, don't get steamed up. Remember your statistical advantage. The same goes for the appointments that slipped your mind and the requests you were asked to comply with but which you forgot. Simply reschedule and say with determination, "This won't happen again," and you'll prove that it really won't.

STEP 3: MOTIVATION FOR THE ADVANCED

Now that we're thinking positively, here's a quick review of what we've learned thus far:

1. Our memory is better than we deem it to be.
2. It's allowed to fail sometimes.
3. If we keep failures in perspective, we won't feel so let down.
4. When we have a positive attitude about our memory, it will surprise us.
5. If we break free of our mental reservations and truly want to enjoy an excellent memory, it will amaze us.

> "If you don't believe in miracles, you're not a realist."
> —DAVID BEN-GURION

When people are highly motivated, even a physical handicap won't hamper their efforts. Have you ever thought about the fact that blind people don't have many auxiliary tools to help them remember? A blind person doesn't take along a written shopping list to the market, since he cannot read it. He has no need for it, either: he has a memory he relies on. When he comes across a friend who's moved recently and asks for his new phone number, he doesn't write it down. He will remember it, as he has no other choice.

Arturo Toscanini, the great conductor, had very poor eyesight for much of his life. The only way for him to conduct the music he loved was to develop a strong memory. Over time, Toscanini learned to conduct entire symphonies without the help of a musical score. One day, a musician came to see the conductor before an important concert and apologized for not being able to perform that evening because his musical instrument had suffered a blow and was no longer capable of producing the G treble clef. Toscanini thought for a moment and said: "You can play. In the composition we're playing tonight there is no G treble clef."

Motivation is not just the desire to improve memory. Efficient motivation, in memory terms, is the desire to remember specific items for defined purposes. All of us are aware of areas in which we are competent and the areas in which we are less so. Decide which area you are especially weak in and start tackling it. Think about the benefits you'll gain. After you accomplish that particular goal, move on to other aspects of your memory.

You could say that until this point I've been treating memory as a commodity and have been trying to sell you your memory back. I have pitched its features, traits, and a few other surprising discoveries to you. However, I haven't gotten to the fun part of the sale yet: telling you what your new "product" will be able to do that others cannot. After you read this book, with your trained memory you will be able to:

- Meet people at an event and remember their names as well as many other facts about them, even years later.
- Remember phone numbers without needing to rely on a phone book.
- Recall information after reading it just once.
- Speak easily in front of an audience without notes, PowerPoint, or other aids.
- Know where you've left something even if your house is a complete mess.
- Remember an appointment scheduled months in advance without sneaking a peek at your calendar.

- Impress your friends with cool memory stunts.
- Win millions of dollars in the lottery. (Okay, this has nothing to do with memory. Never mind.)

You have my word that with your improved memory you'll be able to do all the things I just listed (minus the lottery bit). But in order to truly train your memory, you'll need to train it step by step, and you'll need to practice. First we'll learn a few simple operating principles, after which we'll move on to studying all the techniques that work. With determination and patience, by the time you finish this book, you'll reap the benefits of a stellar memory.

I must emphasize that this isn't like a mystery novel. It will do you no good to turn to the last page in hope of finding out the story's end. Sorry, but the secret to an excellent memory does not lie on the last page alone.

Let's get started.

~~~~~~~~~~~~~~~~~~~~~~~~~~~~~~~~~

CHAPTER 3

YOU SHALL NOT REMEMBER THIS

I PROMISED YOU that you'll be able to perform amazing memory stunts by the time you finish reading this book, and I know you don't really believe me. There's only one way to find out—continue reading and start implementing what you'll be learning.

First, it's necessary to check your memory's current ability so you have a benchmark to compare future results to. The following quizzes aren't scientific, and they aren't as intimidating as the SAT. You don't need to prepare for them by sleeping twelve hours, drinking four cups of coffee, or downing a few chocolate bars.

Don't worry about the results. Most people achieve very low scores at the beginning but then achieve almost perfect scores after having read this book and applied the techniques I'll be explaining. Some of the tasks may seem difficult, if not impossible. If this is the case, it's only because you've never learned how to perform them.

My goal is to help you track your progress as you move along chapter by chapter. With every breakthrough, your confidence in your memory will increase, and you'll be further motivated to continue and succeed.

As tempting as it may be, please don't jump ahead to the next chapter. You won't have many opportunities in life to take an exam where poor performance is expected. Now, grab a pen and a watch, and sit back in a quiet place and relax.

You'll be given a certain memorization task in each quiz. Upon completing the task, do not move on to the next quiz. You will be instructed first to recall what you just memorized in the most accurate manner on an answer sheet that appears later in the chapter. After each quiz, compare your answers and score your results according to the instructions given. Afterward, you can move on to the next quiz.

> "I think animal testing is cruel. They get nervous and get all the answers wrong."
> —STEPHEN FRY

QUIZ #1

In this first quiz you have two tasks: (1) to remember as many words as possible, and (2) to remember them in order.

Study the following list of words for two minutes: *car, rabbit, goulash, clown, pool, elephant, Alka-Seltzer, shirt, kite, deli, television, grass, PC, paintbrush, Viagra, sand, slice of bread, prince.*

NOW GO TO PAGE 25.

QUIZ #2

The following list of words is numbered from 1 to 20. Your aim is to remember these words in the order in which they are presented. Study this list for three minutes.

1. blanket
2. hamburger
3. bicycle
4. steel
5. hippopotamus
6. pizza
7. saucepan
8. hat
9. cucumber
10. hot dog
11. chicken
12. book
13. straw
14. cigarette
15. Bruce Springsteen
16. dough
17. banana
18. cake
19. jam
20. gefilte fish

NOW GO TO PAGE 25.

QUIZ #3

You have one minute to remember the following number in its exact order.

42215172910793504327

NOW GO TO PAGE 26.

QUIZ #4

Here's a list of ten companies or names of people and their phone numbers. The goal is to be able to match the phone number with the name. Study this list for seven minutes.

Ronald McDonaldstein	629-4813
Yankele Obama, Hasidic rapper	544-2903
Napoleon's credit card number	7295431
Bernie Madoff's retirement seminars	4,917,322
DeVito's Delicatessen	629-1133
Anesthesiologists' Awareness Hotline	523-4444
Long John Copper, pirate risk management consultant	291-3402
Muhammed Eli, kosher supervisor	910-2479
Elizabeth and Harry Krishna	677-2880
Jeff and Whoopi Goldblum	512-9797

NOW GO TO PAGE 26.

QUIZ #5

This is the last quiz. Afterward, have a soothing cup of tea, go for a weekend in the Bahamas, and only then come back to this book.

Following is a list of significant dates in history. Review it for two minutes.

1776	The American Revolution
1815	The Battle of Waterloo
1974	Sammy Davis Jr.'s bar mitzvah
1917	The Russian Revolution
1770	Beethoven's birth
1932	Donald Duck's birth
1977	Elvis Presley's death
1969	First man lands on the moon
1986	First woman kissed Sammy Davis Jr.
1948	Prince Charles's birth

NOW, GO TO PAGE 27.

ANSWER SHEET

QUIZ #1

Write down the words you remember in their exact order:

_____

_____

_____

Compare your answers with the original list.

Award yourself one point for each word you remembered and an additional point for every word you remembered in the correct order. If you reversed the order of two items, then they both are incorrect, which means you lose two points. In this quiz, the maximum number of points possible is 40.

YOUR SCORE: _____

QUIZ #2

Write down each word according to its original number on the list.

8_____	14_____
12 _____	2_____
7 _____	11_____
9_____	5_____
3 _____	4_____
6 _____	17_____
18 _____	13_____
15 _____	19_____
20 _____	10_____
1 _____	16_____

Compare your answers to the original list. Award yourself one point for each word that successfully matches its designated number:

YOUR SCORE: _____

QUIZ #3

Write down the entire number in its exact order.

_____

Compare to the original number. Award yourself one point for each digit you remembered successfully in the right sequence.

YOUR SCORE: _____

QUIZ #4

Write down the numbers you remembered below:

Napoleon's credit card number _____

Elizabeth and Harry Krishna _____

Jeff and Whoopi Goldblum _____

DeVito's Delicatessen _____

Muhammed Eli, kosher supervisor_____

Anesthesiologists' Awareness Hotline_____

Long John Copper, pirate risk

    management consultant _____

Ronald McDonaldstein _____

Yankele Obama, Hasidic rapper _____

Bernie Madoff's retirement seminars_____

Check your results. Give yourself 2 points for each success.

YOUR SCORE: _____

QUIZ #5

Write down the year corresponding to each historical event.

_____ Beethoven's birth
_____ The Russian Revolution
_____ First woman kissed Sammy Davis Jr.
_____ Prince Charles's birth
_____ Elvis Presley's death
_____ The American Revolution
_____ Sammy Davis Jr.'s bar mitzvah
_____ The Battle of Waterloo
_____ Donald Duck's birth
_____ First man lands on the moon

Give yourself 2 points for each correct answer.

YOUR SCORE: _____

Track your results with the following chart:

	Maximal score possible	Your score
Quiz 1	40	
Quiz 2	20	
Quiz 3	20	
Quiz 4	20	
Quiz 5	20	
TOTAL	120	

Be aware that the average score is between 25 and 60 points. If you scored higher, you're starting off with a good memory.

After training your brain and putting to use the techniques you'll learn in this book, you'll be able to score between 100 and 120 points—we're talking a 90–95 percent success rate!

How about learning simple and basic principles next, which will provide immediate improvement in your ability to remember things? Yes, you say? Good answer.

PART II

SIMPLE PRINCIPLES FOR TURNING A NORMAL MEMORY INTO A GREAT ONE

WHAT,
WITH THIS BRAIN
YOU THINK
YOU'RE GOING TO
GET INTO
MEDICAL SCHOOL?

CHAPTER 4

〰〰〰〰〰〰〰〰〰〰〰〰〰〰〰〰〰〰〰

HAVE YOU SEEN
MY HEAD?

It Was on My Shoulders a Minute Ago!

THE BRAIN IS A WONDERFUL ORGAN. IT BEGINS WORKING
THE MOMENT YOU GET UP IN THE MORNING AND DOES
NOT STOP UNTIL YOU GET INTO THE OFFICE.
—*Abraham Lincoln, 1958*

EVERY DAY WE see the same things dozens, if not hundreds, of
times. Yet when asked to recall them, our memory suddenly
conks out.

Traveling from Antwerp, Belgium, to Paris by train several
years ago, a fifty-year-old businessman named Samuel Goldman sat down next to me. While talking about Jerusalem, a
place he had last visited eight years earlier, he was reminded
of a small playground he saw at the intersection of Herzog
and Tchernichovsky Streets. At the time, I lived in that very

neighborhood, and if there was one thing that I was positive was *not* there, it was a playground.

"Pardon me," I said with a smile, "but I believe you're mistaken."

"No, I'm not," Samuel insisted. "If you come by way of Rupin Avenue, you can't miss it."

Samuel's self-confidence irritated me, so I took out my cell phone and placed it on the small table in front of us.

"I'm going to call my daughter right now to find out which one of us is right. Would you like to wager anything before I call her?"

Samuel nodded and smiled. "A cup of coffee when we reach Paris will be fine."

"You've got a deal," I answered. "I'll enjoy that cup of coffee."

I called my daughter.

"Gali, dear," I said, gazing at Samuel with a smirk, "At the intersection of Herzog and Tchernichovsky, across from the Monastery of the Holy Cross, is there a playground? I made a bet with someone."

Gali was quiet for a moment.

"Of course there is, Daddy," she replied. "But you never take me there."

"Wow," I said, ending the call and lowering my eyes in defeat. "I can't believe I didn't remember that."

Samuel gave me a kind, reassuring smile.

"It's only natural," he explained. "Your senses become numbed to the things in your everyday environment, and you no longer notice them."

Upon arrival in Paris, we headed for a coffee shop. Samuel drew my attention to a colorful illumination on one of the rooftops.

"You really notice everything, don't you?" I complimented him.

Samuel smiled. A hint of sadness was apparent in that smile.

"It's merely my Jewish survival instinct." He adjusted his coat uneasily. "My father opened his first jewelry store in Antwerp," he went on. "I would stand next to him in the shop, and as each customer entered, my father would correctly guess where the man was from, what he did for a living, and if he was married or not. All this with just a quick glance. He was the one who came up with the term 'Jewish survival instinct.' My father claimed that, as a persecuted Jew who was alienated wherever he went throughout his entire life, he developed an instinct to pay close attention to the smallest details and assign them greater importance."

Maybe it's because we live safe, comfortable lives or maybe it's because we're overwhelmed with information, but the disturbing fact is that our collective level of attention and concentration has radically decreased in the past twenty years. We hardly notice anything anymore. In my lectures I ask participants to draw the logos of famous brands. Take Burger King's, for example. How many times have you seen that logo? Yet, are you able to draw it?

Before you say "sure," grab a pen and a piece of paper and draw the Burger King logo as it appears on all of the company's products—but do this accurately.

What did you come up with? Maybe a drawing of a crown, or a *B*, or a hamburger?

And what about Starbucks, 7-Eleven, and Pizza Hut? Can you recall their logos in detail?

Most people will not be able to accurately describe them, though they've seen them countless times. (An unusual exception was a teenager who attended one of my seminars. Not only did he draw the logo of Pizza Hut on the white-board, he also added the toll-free phone number for orders, to everyone's amusement.)

So why don't we remember logos we've seen hundreds of times? Because we never really pay attention to them from the get-go. For another example, think about Leonardo da Vinci's famous painting of the Mona Lisa. Can you re-call what's to the left of her in the painting? Probably not, though you've seen her image many times. I won't keep you in suspense—there's a yellow river leading to a lake.

This chapter opens with a humorous quote. Did you notice the two errors in the attribution? The first may be difficult. It was Robert Frost who said those words, not Lincoln. But even if it had been Lincoln, did you notice the date following his name? In 1958 Lincoln had been in his grave for nearly a century.

The basic problem with memory is lack of attention. We'll never be able to remember something if we don't pay atten-tion to it to begin with. We hear, but we do not listen. We see, but we do not observe. In other words, we focus on a few things that catch our interest and neglect the total picture.

> My wife always com-plains I never listen to her . . . or something like that.

After the logo test, frustration settles in among my seminar par-ticipants and many become defen-sive: "Why should I pay attention to—and remember—what Burger King's logo looks like? Who even cares?"

Granted, it may be that it isn't really important to remem-ber company logos, though fortunes are spent designing them. But you do want to remember Allan's name five years from now when you run into him on the street, or where you put the car keys you just had in your hand. All it takes is one second of attention—that's it.

The memorizing process can be divided into three parts:

Stage 1: Absorbing the information
Stage 2: Storing or filing the information in our memory
Stage 3: Extracting this information

But most of us don't even get past the first step! Imagine that you're at a cocktail party and your good friend Dr. Mark Jones suddenly grabs your sleeve. "Come over here a second," he says. "I have to introduce you to someone." He leads you to a person who seems as caught off guard as you, and makes the introduction. "This is Roger Waterhouse—the guy I told you about. He got me that book about helping your cat to think outside the box."

You extend a hand and, with a forced smile, say: "Yes, Mark told me about you. Actually I used to have a white Persian cat who thought outside the box. He's a tiger now. Maybe you saw him in Siegfried and Roy's show in Vegas."

The conversation continues for a bit and eventually ends. The question, though, is what did you do with Roger Waterhouse's name once you were introduced? Nothing! It went in one ear and out the other, failing to be absorbed.

It's important to be aware of this natural tendency, When you're introduced to an unfamiliar person's name, keep in mind that you must remember it. (Later in this book, you'll learn how to store names in memory in such a way that you'll be able to recall them years from now.)

I liken this to working on a PC. When composing a document, we save the file as we work on it and again when we are done. If we fail to click on Save once before we close the document, we'll have to start all over again. The second it takes to click on Save and store the document under the appropriate file name is that second of awareness I am talking about. Until we decide once and for all to save a name in our memory, we'll need to ask a person for his name over and over again.

The same goes with something I like to call "locked door syndrome." You know the drill—you leave home and, well into the journey, you start to wonder: "Did I lock the door? Yikes, I hope I remembered to unplug the iron too."

Develop a simple habit: each time you exit your home, lock the door, jiggle the doorknob twice, and say *out loud*: "I've locked the door. I know the door is locked." Yes, someone might see you, and you might end up spending some nice vacation time in a special place for the mentally disturbed . . . but at least you'll know your home is locked and safe.

It seems that there are hundreds of ways in which our memory might fail. The truth is, there are only three:

1. We might fail in absorbing the new information. ("You talkin' to me?")
2. We might fail in saving the information, similar to saving a document on a PC. ("Harry, did you remember to take out the garbage before we left for Australia?")
3. We might fail in retrieving the information once we've saved it. ("Now where did I put Kennedy's secret photos of Marilyn? Perhaps in the 'Cuban Missile' file . . .")

EFFECTIVE ABSORBING MEANS PAYING ATTENTION

Are you familiar with the famous story about the absent-minded professor who, upon leaving his house every morning, pats his wife and kisses the dog? We usually tag this phenomenon as "distraction" or "lack of concentration." But it's really lack of attention.

This happens to all of us. We enter a room and forget why we went in there in the first place. We say we're sorry to a mannequin we bump into at Macy's. Once, in a moment of complete lack of concentration, I happened to thank the ATM after drawing out cash.

In a world drowning with information overload and distractions, how can we possibly improve our concentration skills when so many of us have ADD, ADHD, or a PhD?

> "My grandfather loved to give me advice but was a little forgetful. One day he took me aside and left me there."
> —RON RICHARDS

There are two ways to improve them—by elevating our level of attention and by distributing it correctly.

ELEVATING YOUR LEVEL OF ATTENTION

Can you guess how many people on this planet experience attention deficit disorder (ADD) to some degree? How many have trouble concentrating for long periods of time and suffer from memory problems of one kind or another?

Here is the comforting truth—it's *everyone*. We all have a limited attention span! Even the greatest superheroes—Superman, Spider-Man, Schneiderman, and Batman—have this problem. There are always those two seconds when their attention lapses and their enemies gain the upper hand. The good news is that we don't have their kinds of enemies, and there is something we can do about the "lack of attention" foe.

In the previous chapter we talked about motivation for remembering. What would it take to motivate you to enhance your attention skills?

There are some professions where the number one

motivation to develop superb attention skills is simple to define: to keep the job. Take air traffic controllers. For them, paying attention is a crucial requirement.

> Boss: "Jerry, did you remember to instruct Air France
> 431 and KLM 1034 to reposition their altitudes?"
> Jerry: "Oh, gee, sorry, boss. I guess I didn't. I must have
> had a senior moment."
> Boss: "Well, I guess that explains why they disappeared
> from radar."

Imagine a detective who doesn't notice small details: that the car parked out front has a different license plate, or that a suspect's heels are higher than usual. It's just a matter of time before he's searching for a new job. Detectives and security officers learn how to increase their ability to pay attention to details. We can too.

Play a little detective game. When you next walk down a busy street, try to isolate the noise coming from traffic and pay attention to other sounds, such as people's conversations, music from a radio, or birds chirping. If you go to a concert, try to concentrate on the music coming from specific instruments.

Many ancient Eastern practices, such as martial arts, origami (Japanese paper folding), ikebana (Japanese flower arranging), and calligraphy, assist in developing concentration and attention skills. In fact, research indicates that origami also helps develop associative thinking skills and patience.

DISTRIBUTING ATTENTION CORRECTLY

I have friends who, unlike me, have wonderful recall of details from movies we've seen together—they're even able to recite complete lines. Does this mean that their memory is better than mine? No. It means that when it comes to films, their observation and attention abilities are better than mine. This is my specific "malfunction" in that area. While I focus on the general plot, they focus on conversations, noticing minute details.

Sometimes it's possible to find amusing errors in films. Have you ever noticed a microphone boom bobbing around the top of the movie frame on the screen? Oops. The classic film *Ben-Hur*, starring Charlton Heston, takes place during the Roman era. Yet you can see one of the extras wearing a fancy Rolex, which even Julius Caesar didn't own at the time.

It isn't enough simply to pay attention; it's necessary to distribute your attention properly. Back to the party where Dr. Jones introduced us to Roger Waterhouse, standing next to Roger was his wife, who introduced herself as well. What was her name? Who are you kidding? If you didn't bother to remember Roger Waterhouse, how the heck are you going to remember his wife?

While chatting in a group, it's natural to skip from one person to another every few minutes, dividing your attention among them. However—and this is crucial—when you're talking to someone, focus on that person. Devote your entire attention to her, and don't allow others to distract you. Be aware that you need to concentrate on the person you're conversing with at that moment. We've all been on the other side and know how annoying and insulting it is when we talk with someone and he has that glazed look in his eyes. You know he's not listening.

But if you apply this technique, the next time you arrive at a noisy party, something refreshing will happen. Instead of being frustrated with your inability to follow the many people and conversations, you'll be able to remember each person and what each one of them said.

In the future, when you run into Susan (Roger's wife), instead of trying to remember why she looks so familiar, you'll surprise her with your good memory and ask her how that new Microsoft deal is going. (It turns out that Susan is the CEO of a start-up firm that recently signed a multimillion-dollar deal with the giant corporation.)

Attention is the most important element of memory. Paying attention to details will solve many memory frustrations, even before you learn additional techniques. This will become as conditioned a habit as the instinct to make sure your wallet is in your pocket or your purse is closed.

How about one more surprise for your "motivation collection"? Believe it or not, it's been scientifically proven that paying attention generates luck. Remember Samuel Goldman's father's advice: "Pay close attention to the smallest details and assign them greater importance." Well, Richard Wiseman, author of *The Luck Factor*, studied the differences between people who claimed they were lucky in life and those who grumbled about being unlucky. His conclusion is that lucky people are those who keep an open mind, pay attention to things, and take advantage of opportunities.

So let's get lucky and learn how to easily make things noticeable and memorable.

~~~~~~~~~~~~~~~~~~~~~~~~~

CHAPTER 5

THAT REMINDS ME OF STRASBOURG

I KNOW MOTHER-IN-LAW clichés are out of fashion, and it's not nice to make fun of these lovely ladies, but for educational purposes I need to tell you about my very own mother-in-law.

When I first met her, she told me about her childhood in Strasbourg, France. This is totally acceptable for a first date with your potential in-laws. One should get to know them in order to assess how your future wife or husband might turn out to be.

However, twenty years have passed and Strasbourg still remains the main theme of our Shabbat dinners. No matter what topic we bring to the table, the evening won't go by without a story about Strasbourg.

Here is an example of a typical Shabbat dinner conversation, right after we bless the food:

Me: "The watermelons are very good this year."

She: "My friend Natalie wrote from Strasbourg. She still lives there, you know."

Me: "What does this have to do with watermelons?"

A week later:

Me: "I read a disturbing article about penguins and global warming. They are quite miserable, those poor penguins."

She: "Yes, so sad, but I am surprised how efficient the trams were in Strasbourg. I understand that the number 23 still runs to the cathedral."

Let me clarify that she is a wonderful woman and we get along very well. It's Strasbourg that drives me crazy.

There's always a reason why someone brings up a different topic while in conversation. I like to call it "association disorder." For my mother-in-law, something I say reminds her of a completely different subject, triggered by association to a word, sentence, or idea she just heard. Association guides our memory, and everything we remember is associated with something else.

I once tried to analyze my mother-in-law's way of thinking. This is probably how it works: global warming = penguins = snow = Strasbourg in the winter = cold wind on the street = need to warm up = get on tram = tram 23 = final stop at the cathedral. And there you have it: the connection between penguins and cathedrals.

Associations can be expressed in all forms and through all our senses. If you come across a man with a black mustache, he may remind you of Burt Reynolds (or Stalin, I suppose, if you're having a particularly bad day). A similar phenomenon explains why you called Bill, the new guy at work, Simon. That's because he looks a lot like the Simon you know.

If you're asked to draw a map of Belgium or Finland, it's likely that you won't be able to replicate their outlines, even though you've seen their general shapes in the world atlas. But if you are asked to draw Italy, you'll probably be able to do so, because Italy's form is more memorable, as it resembles a boot.

The national anthem may remind you of the Super Bowl. An Elvis Presley, Bee Gees, or George Michael ballad may evoke nostalgic memories of first love, your teenage years, or even certain people who liked these performers.

Scents evoke strong memories as well. Lilacs may remind you of your prom. Suntan lotion ignites the memory of summer on the beach. The aroma of apple pie brings back warm memories of Grandma's house; the smell of burnt apple pie can remind us that, well, perhaps Grandma wasn't such a great baker.

THE POWER OF ASSOCIATIVE MEMORY PRESERVATION

Most of us instinctively use associations to help us remember different things. Let's say that the PIN for your ATM card is 1392. Perhaps 13 is a reminder of someone's birthday, who was born on the thirteenth of April, and your favorite car was a 1992 model.

But how can we remember things that don't share a commonality or are not related to anything else we know?

To our rescue comes a trait that distinguishes us from computers—the ability to imagine. With all due respect, a computer simply does not have an imagination. We, on the other hand, have a well-developed imagination on several levels.

In the eleventh century, Yehuda Halevi, a prominent rabbi and philosopher, spoke with the king of the Khazars, a semi-nomadic Turkic people, about two related powers: the power of visualization and the power of preservation. When a person wants to remember something, he instructs his imagination to conjure up images and scenarios that are engraved in his soul and kept there by the power of preservation. If he wants to remember the miraculous revelation at Mount Sinai, all he has to do is imagine he's standing there with the people of Israel, Moses cradling the Ten Commandments. The more active the imagination, the more a person becomes a participant in that historical moment.

The ancient Greeks also understood this, and indicated that the two elements on which a functioning memory is based are association and imagination. However, the Jews, who were the founding fathers of this concept, emphasized that if you really want to remember something you need to create powerful, wild, and extraordinary pictures in your mind. Actually, it was the Holy One who bestowed the gift of powerful imagination on the people of Israel. In the book of Exodus, He commands all of Israel, "Remember this day, in which you came out from Egypt."

Now, since the Lord knows that His people don't have the greatest memory, He taught them techniques: "By the signs and the paragons." He meant occurrences that leave an unforgettable impression, such as all the plagues of Egypt— blood, locusts, lice, hail, as well as the death of the firstborn. In other words, God basically tells the people of Israel, "Imagine the plagues that I inflicted on Egypt and let this remind you who is the truest and greatest God of them all."

All the methods and techniques later developed by the Greeks, Romans, and memory entertainers are based on these two factors: associative links created by strongly imaginative pictures. I don't assume that a person with an untrained memory will be able to remember a list of ten items, in order, after hearing or seeing it only once. But with a little bit of effort you'll be able to do this. All you have to do right now is to shift your imagination into high gear. You are about to introduce the most ridiculous, absurd, and illogical images to your mind's eye.

Take note of the following:

bed
eel
flowerpot
watermelon
candle
frying pan
orange
car
hippo
skirt

As you go over the words in the list, take a mental photograph of each one on its own. The goal is to create a succession of pictures related to one another. The image in your mind must be clear and fully detailed. For example, if I tell you to imagine a car, it's important you know what kind of car we are talking about. Is it a Buick or a Mazda? Is it a convertible or an SUV?

Now you must use your senses in a new way. You need to learn to exchange them, or rather, to share them. The tongue senses flavors and the eyes see colors. When the eyes see honey, the mind imagines its sweetness, just as when the eyes see snow, a cold sensation can send shivers through your body. One sense leads to the other. The key to remembering this list is to *create a chain of images that will lead from one to the other.*

For practice, I'll give you an example of how intensely our imagination can affect our senses. Visualize the following scene vividly as you read.

> You're holding a Styrofoam cup in your hand. Imagine the way it feels with your fingers. Squeeze it lightly and sense its smoothness and flexibility, but be careful not to break the cup. Place it on the kitchen counter. Open a jar of your favorite instant coffee. Inhale its intoxicating aroma. Now, pick up a shiny silver spoon and scoop up some coffee with it. Slowly move the spoon over the cup and empty its contents inside. Listen to the cascading sound of the granules as they slide into the cup, settling at the bottom. Now lift the cup to the spout of the hot water urn and pull down the lever. Listen to the sound of the hot water as it fills the cup; take note of the steam swirling above. Look at the bubbles and foam created as solid turns into liquid.
>
> Take a salt shaker (yes, a salt shaker) and pour its contents inside the cup. Stir the water and salt using your spoon. Lift up the cup to your lips. Take a small sip of the hot, steaming, salty liquid.

Did you purse your lips in disgust? Did you sense the halting saltiness? Did you have the urge to wash this awful taste out of your mouth?

The difference between imagination and reality is minute. The body responds physiologically to a richly imagined thought as if it were real. The resulting reaction is instinctive. The more quickly you learn to imagine with all of your senses, the faster your memory will improve.

MEMORY IN LIVING COLOR

The person noted for having the best memory the world has ever known was a Russian named Solomon Shereshevskii. He remembered everything using associative techniques based on his wild imagination.

In 1920 the Soviet psychologist A. L. Luria began to study Shereshevskii's incredible memory and discovered that his secret was based on the same ancient Jewish technique—an intensified application of sense sharing. Shereshevskii would see colors when he heard music. He could smell voices, too, along with many other weird talents. For example, when talking with the renowned psychologist L. S. Vygotsky, Shereshevskii exclaimed, "What a crumbling, yellow voice you have!" Scientists call this *synesthesia* (from the Greek *syn*, "together," and *aisthesis*, "perception"—literally, "joined perception"), a neurologically based phenomenon in which stimulation of one sense leads to automatic, involuntary experiences in a second sense. Shereshevskii remembered the list of meaningless words that he had recited to Luria by creating images using measurements and flavors. He even remembered how to get to the research institute in Moscow by imagining the salty "taste" of the bricks in the wall that led there.

Shereshevskii's synesthetic abilities gave him a tremendous memory, but I believe that even people who are not born with this trait can do something similar.

Let's go back to the list of words I asked you to remember and see how sharing senses can help with this process.

Imagine the first word—*bed*. We all know what a bed looks like, so think about your own bed. Picture the bed's frame, the mattress, or the sheets on it right now. Try to imagine this as clearly as possible.

Now on to the next word—*eel*. Taking the first step toward a trained memory, we'll create a link between the word *bed*, now implanted in our memory, and *eel*. The link between the two images must be as absurd as possible. For example, imagine that a giant slimy eel is sleeping in your cozy bed—a pretty awful thought, isn't it? Very good. This is an image you will remember well. The reason I asked you to imagine such a ridiculous thing is because we have a tendency to better remember the absurd and illogical. A logical image isn't as interesting, so we don't engrave it in our memory. Close your eyes to imagine the scene clearly.

The minute you have taken a mental photograph of the eel in your bed, move on to the next word, *flowerpot*. Concentrate on connecting *eel* and *flowerpot*. Say you imagine that the giant slimy eel—twelve feet long and now well rested—sticks out of one of your flowerpots. Its head is in the soil and its tail is flapping up in the air. "Smell" the slimy eel as if it were a stinky flower. Can you picture this image in your mind?

Moving on to *watermelon*, let's create a new link between *flowerpot* and *watermelon*. Imagine that you have a watermelon-shaped flowerpot. It's round and green on the outside and has an opening at the top, and yet the red fruit inside is gone. Instead, it's filled with brown soil, out of which grows a flowering plant. If you wish, you may place this unique flowerpot next to one containing the eel. I'm sorry for nagging, but you must imagine this detailed image. You don't need to spend fifteen minutes finding the most absurd images possible; just mentally photograph the first vision that pops into your head. If you conjure up two possible images, go with the stronger of the two—meaning the stranger one.

Now on to *candle*. Let's connect *watermelon* with *candle*. This is easy. Imagine a long candle stuck inside a watermelon, or a giant watermelon-shaped candle, wick on top.

Frying pan is next, which we'll link to *candle*. Imagine our fruity candle is used to cook up some scrambled eggs. Think about a frying pan, place it above the candle in the living room, and get cooking. Imagine a strong flame rising from the candle.

Moving on to *orange*, take the *frying pan* (after you've eaten the eggs, of course) and use it as a tennis racket. Start lobbing hundreds of oranges everywhere. Watch the flying fruit cause great destruction around your house; one orange shatters a vase, while another strikes the lamp.

Don't try to remember the previous items. Just focus on the vision of the image I'm currently describing to you.

We're up to *car*, so picture four large *oranges* as the wheels of a fancy Mercedes. Focus on the car cruising down the street on these four oranges. Notice the contrast between the citrusy tires and the body of the luxury car, which is a sleek silver.

Now let's upgrade our senses and think like Shereshevskii. Try to imagine that the Mercedes tastes like orange juice. Can you do that? Lick the car's hood in your imagination and feel the tangy taste of orange. Try it for several seconds.

From *car* we go to *hippo*. Inside this fancy Mercedes sits a hippopotamus, one foreleg on the steering wheel and the other resting on the open window. Envision the proud look on the hippo's face. Now smell the hippo, but imagine he has skin like the leather upholstery in fancy cars. Can you smell the high-end hippo?

We have reached the last word, *skirt*. Imagine yourself walking down the street when suddenly you spot a *hippo* wearing a pink miniskirt. We're talking about a male hippo here (who seems to have a serious identity crisis—otherwise he would be wearing jeans, like any normal male hippo). See the skirt flapping in the wind. Listen to the noises the hippo makes as he struts down the street.

Let's find out what we remember now that we've completed the list.

The first word was *bed*. In the future, in order to remember the first word in a certain list, associate it with something else. In this case, let's imagine that we're balancing the bed on our head (like African women who balance large baskets on their noggins).

What was sleeping in our bed?

An *eel*.

Where did the eel get stuck? In the *flowerpot*.

And what was different about this flowerpot? It was shaped like a *watermelon*.

And this watermelon wasn't really a watermelon—it was actually a *candle*.

And this candle, with its flickering flame, was used to heat up a *frying pan*.

With this frying pan, we played tennis using *oranges* as tennis balls.

What "tasted" orange? A *car*.

Who was driving the car? A *hippo*.

Who then strolled down the street wearing a *skirt*.

You have just remembered a random ten-word list.

Write down this list on the next page now without guidance.

WHERE DID NOAH PARK THE ARK?

If you didn't remember a particular word, or even more than one, don't worry. It just means that the association wasn't strong enough and the image wasn't fully imbedded in your memory—perhaps you don't like cross-dressing hippos. Just strengthen this loose link using an image you prefer, and go over the list again. I do believe you were able to remember most of the list, including other facts as well.

What type was the car? A Mercedes—right!

What was frying in the pan? Eggs.

Do you remember what kind? Scrambled or sunny side up? Scrambled—right again!

Most of us were raised to think logically, and here I am, asking you to create illogical images and share your senses. It may be challenging to conjure up such images, but after you've done so a few times, you'll find out that it's easier than you thought.

Here are some simple rules to help you create strong, effective associations:

1. Imagine the item in abnormal proportions—too big or too small (a giant eel sleeping in your bed).
2. Imagine the item in action (a Mercedes cruising by on four oranges).
3. Switch between items (a watermelon instead of a flowerpot).
4. Exaggerate the amount (hundreds of oranges flying around).
5. Use your senses:

   Sight. Make special use of vivid colors (oranges replacing wheels, a bright candle stuck in a watermelon).
   Sound. Listen to the sound of oranges hitting the frying pan.

Smell. Smell the eel.

Taste. Taste the orange juice flavor of the car.

Touch. Touch the smooth watermelon, the orange's rough peel.

6. Exchange senses (balance a bed on your head, listen to the sound of the skirt).

Most important, create images that are as ridiculous and as absurd as possible. Upgrade your imagination and think wild.

The association method can be used as a tool to remember your daily schedule, a speech, or what's going to be on a test, for example. If you'd like to implement it right away, you can use it to memorize a shopping list. Or impress your friends with a memory stunt—ask them to read you a list of twenty to thirty words, and repeat it back to them from beginning to end (or from end to beginning).

Just a friendly word of caution: The next time you order pizza, don't ask if it sounds happy and can be ordered with extra comical cheese. Nor should you reveal your new fetish for licking the hoods of Mercedes cars.

But most important, if you ever travel to Strasbourg, be sure to make time to visit the penguins at the cathedral.

CHAPTER 6

BREAKING NEWS:
THE GREATEST MEMORY
SECRET . . . REVEALED!

ALWAYS GET MARRIED EARLY IN THE MORNING.
THAT WAY, IF IT DOESN'T WORK OUT,
YOU HAVEN'T WASTED A WHOLE DAY.
—*Mickey Rooney*

THERE'S A TEST I like to conduct during my lectures that always brings a smile to the participants' faces. I invite two or three couples onstage, men in front, women behind them, and ask each man to describe exactly what his spouse or girlfriend is wearing: shirt, pants or skirt, jacket, socks, shoes, earrings, necklaces, rings . . . This usually elicits some good laughs, because most men are far from correct when describing what their partners are wearing.

Why do men fail this test? Because the details of what someone is wearing don't interest them. Ladies, I don't know how to break this to you, but you're wasting your time and

54

money. Men couldn't really care less about clothes and fashion (well, most of them, anyway).

On the other hand, many women complain about their deteriorating memory but can remember precisely what they wore to a certain party three years ago. What's the worst thing that can happen at a party, fashion-wise? A woman sees another woman wearing the same dress that she is wearing. Catastrophe! The two women won't speak. But when a man sees another man with a shirt exactly like his, they become best friends for the rest of their lives.

> "When I grow up I want to be a little boy."
> —JOSEPH HELLER

Some parents complain to me about their kid's lousy memory—that he doesn't remember anything at school and gets bad grades. Miraculously, however, the same child has excellent recall for the names of his favorite football players, can sing all the lyrics to his favorite pop songs, and can recite verbatim all the lines from a movie he's seen umpteen times.

Why? Because we'll always better remember the things that interest us, just as we usually fail to remember what we don't care about. Those who easily remember names and faces are genuinely interested in people. Those who remember phone numbers, serial numbers, license plates, and catalog numbers usually have good mathematical or technical skills. And those who are talented with trivia possess a high level of curiosity about a broad range of subjects.

Older folk frequently complain that they vividly remember events that happened thirty years ago but totally forget what happened yesterday. The reason for this is not biological—it's much more distressing. When we were young, everything was new and exciting. We used to ask, "Why is the sky blue?" or "Where do babies come from?" As we've advanced in our years, our questions have shifted to "Why didn't you call?" "Who's your lawyer?" and "What in the world does she see in him?" As we age, we become skeptical, cynical, and intellectually "impaired"—we think we've seen everything, heard everything, and know everything. Nothing becomes engraved in our memory the same way it was in our youth.

So here it is, the greatest memory secret of all, the one characteristic that will help your recall, prevent forgetfulness, and lead to a wonderful life: *enthusiasm*. Be enthusiastic in your daily life. Let the smallest things excite you. You'll discover how easily you remember things and how the quality of your life improves dramatically.

I have two close friends who are perfect examples of how interest and passion play a crucial role in memory. I'll call them Susan and Alfred. They're senior citizens, and both are physically and mentally in great shape; however, Susan hardly forgets things, while Alfred constantly does.

They once went on a trip to Italy. Upon their return, Susan bubbled with enthusiasm to share her experiences. She told me in great detail about the works of the artists Caravaggio and Modigliani, and Bernini's famed sculptures.

"Wow, you really remember all those artists?" Alfred exclaimed with admiration. "I can't even remember one name."

"That's because you spent most of your time looking for museum coffee shops," Susan replied.

"Yes," he said with a smile. "That I remember well. Anyway, I don't like walking too much. It hurts, you know."

"What hurts?" I asked, knowing Alfred was a constant complainer.

"Well, everything hurts," he replied, waving a hand dismissively. "And what doesn't hurt doesn't really work anymore."

Which just goes to show that attitude, interest, and passion play a major role in how much we will remember—or forget.

Historically, an enthusiast was a person with a belief in religious inspiration accompanied by strong emotions. There was actually a Syrian sect during the fourth century known as the Enthusiasts—they believed that through perpetual prayer and ecstatic practices, believers could be inspired by the Holy Spirit. But being religious isn't a prerequisite for finding reasons to be enthusiastic about life. Each and every one of us houses passion in our hearts for at least one thing. Perhaps not with the same intensity as it once did, or it's shifted to other areas of interest, but it's there, and can be easily sparked again.

Here's a little exercise that will help you relight that inner flame. As you answer the following questions, pay attention to the way they make you feel.

Write down a list of things you were once passionate about (a certain sports team, a performer, a hobby, etc.):

_____

Now write down what interests you today (grandchildren, traveling, etc.):

_____

Think back to your high school days. Recall three positive events from that time:

_____

Recount a positive experience from the past month or two:

_____

What excites and interests you in your life today? (If the answer is nothing, don't be discouraged—just continue reading.)

_____

How can we remember something that doesn't interest us?

> "Take an interest in your husband's activities—hire a detective."
> —BUMPER STICKER

It's important to realize that as you become more familiar with a subject, you take greater interest in it. Say a kid who has never collected stamps gets a few as a gift. This kid will show some initial interest, even only if out of politeness. Now let's say that a week later, his father buys him a pack of a hundred stamps and an album. Most likely this kid will respond with great enthusiasm.

What if you have to study an incredibly boring subject? The way to do this is by "attacking" it on two fronts:

1. Begin with the part that could interest you, then go on to learn what's mandatory.
2. Find the usefulness in studying that subject.

Let's say you have to study automotive mechanics, but you have no idea how a car is built. Even the very thought of having to study this makes eating lima beans seem very appealing. After stumbling through the introduction in the textbook, you get to the first chapter, titled "Automobile Structure," and you quickly close the book, opting to head to the kitchen for those beans. But before you take such drastic measures, think for a moment: "Is there anything about cars that may actually interest me?" Perhaps you're interested in luxury stretch limousines, or finding out about the fastest car in the world, or the first car ever built.

Once you browse through that daunting textbook and find something of interest, go back to the first chapter. You won't grumble nearly as much; you may even find that you're compelled to read on and learn some other car factoids.

Try to remember the first time you met some of your

friends. What was the first impression they made? Could it be that they even seemed boring at first? Only after getting to know them better did you discover they were interesting and downright enchanting. Knowledge creates interest, and interest leads to more knowledge—so it goes.

"WHAT'S IN IT FOR ME?": GENERATING INCENTIVES

Need an incentive to be a great student? Check out the tempting one religious Jews face when they're young adults.

In many Torah-observant circles, the custom of *shidduchim* (matchmaking) still prevails. Young men and women do not really mingle socially and are educated separately from grade school on up. They also usually marry with the assistance of a professional matchmaker. This matchmaker takes several factors into consideration when trying to pair up a couple, including family status, income, looks, personality, and—please note—brains! To make a long story short, if you're the brightest student in the yeshiva, chances are you'll get to pick from the cream of the crop—girls with beauty and big allowances. Can you imagine a greater incentive to succeed? If someone told me during my college days that getting high grades would get me a date with the most beautiful girl on campus, I would have definitely tried much harder. (Actually, I got to marry the most beautiful

A matchmaker knocked on the door of a stubborn bachelor.

"I don't need your help," the young man said. "I will marry for love."

"It's of love that I wish to speak," the matchmaker replied. "We're talking about the only daughter of a very rich man. Her uncle on her father's side has no children, so all his fortune will go to her. The widowed aunt has also left everything in her will to the girl. How could one possibly not love such a girl?"

girl on campus. She, however, was not my prize. I was her punishment.)

Humans simply need a variety of incentives to motivate and prompt us to learn something seemingly uninteresting and complicated.

Maybe you can't stand chemistry, but you need to learn it. A creative solution to this "problem" could be the ability to concoct your own perfume with your newfound knowledge. You could call it Debbie Givenchy, and after establishing your first storefront, you could become the owner of a wildly popular and lucrative boutique perfume chain.

Does the financial section of the paper bore you? Would you rather sit in the dentist's chair for hours than attend the finance class required for your business degree? Well, think of the benefits of knowing the difference between effective and nominal interest rates. Armed with such important information, no bank will be able to convince you that a specific loan is attractive when it's obviously not. Then you'll raise your glass and toast: "To our friend the banker—may he never lose interest!"

What happens when, no matter how hard you try, you can't get charged up about something you've got to learn? This is when you have to determine an artificial benefit.

> "Tell me and I'll forget; show me and I may remember; involve me and I'll understand."
> —CHINESE PROVERB

The Maharal of Prague, the great sixteenth-century Talmudic scholar and mystic, called it "sugarcoating." You need to entice yourself, or a student you're teaching, with small incentives. Some scholars I've spoken with remember their rabbi placing a chocolate bar by the Hebrew alphabet sign at the front of the classroom when they were children. Every time they answered him correctly, they were rewarded with a tasty square. (Kind of reminds one of Sea World, but I guess if it works for dolphins, it'll work for humans.)

Say you're majoring in history at college. In order to graduate you have to take a compulsory course, "The Changes in Louis the 68th's Attitude Toward Claude the 29th's Mother in the Face of Her Refusal to Allow Philip the 19th to Plant Tulips at Versailles During the Summer of 1684." It just so happens that this course is based on the thesis of the department head, who truly believes that this was one of the most important chapters in French history. He holds that this is what caused the eventual banishment of Napoleon to St. Helena. While you may resent this curriculum requirement all you wish, there's no escaping the need to study subjects that you take little or no interest in as you journey toward obtaining that glorious degree.

You may need to force yourself to listen to your professor drone on, or to read a painfully boring article. The way to hang in there is to pin your hopes on a reward—like a hot fudge sundae when the class ends. If it turns out that during the course of one month you've eaten twelve sundaes, you may want to seriously consider switching your major . . . and joining Weight Watchers.

Negative incentives can also help you accomplish a certain task. One of the most famous directives for a Jew to remember his past and traditions is found in the Torah: "If I forget thee, O Jerusalem, may my right hand become lame." Tell yourself that if you don't get through the next three chapters of this book, you are prohibited from watching the finals of your favorite sporting event. (No one should be subjected to such cruelty.)

BONUS: THE TALMUDIC SECRET TO WISDOM
IN A NUTSHELL

Most people enjoy enlightening others with their knowledge and self-proclaimed expertise. "Be humble," the Talmud suggests. "The words of the Torah exist only for those whose opinions are meek." It continues, "Every arrogant man, even if he is smart—his wisdom abandons him."

Rabbi Hanina likened studying Torah to water. Water flows from a high spot to a low one. In the same manner, only a modest person can learn new things. The boastful person hears only himself and thinks that he knows everything. If he thinks he knows everything, then he doesn't learn new things, and he certainly never reviews the old. In either case, "his wisdom abandons him." However, a modest and humble person feels no need to prove himself. His main concern is to listen and learn new things.

Be humble, find interest in unexpected places, and generate enthusiasm in your life. Not only will you remember better, people will remember you as a great human being.

~~~~~~~~~~~~~~~~~~~~~~~~~~~~~~~~

CHAPTER 7

DON'T AGONIZE— ORGANIZE

ORGANIZING IS WHAT YOU DO BEFORE YOU DO SOMETHING,
SO THAT WHEN YOU DO IT, IT IS NOT ALL MIXED UP.
—*Winnie the Pooh*

WE'VE DISCUSSED HOW the human brain's memorizing process is similar to the process in which a computer stores information. This resemblance is also related to the way we need to organize the information for effective retrieval.

Think what would happen if you saved a report you painstakingly wrote on your computer without giving it a title or assigning it a folder. When the time came to find it, you'd have to scan through all your files without any guarantee that you'd succeed. Whatever we want to remember must be organized in our brain—like in a computer—for optimal effectiveness and future retrieval.

Religious texts are an example of masterly organization. The Old Testament is divided into chapters and verses—more specifically, 39 books, 929 chapters, 23,214 paragraphs, and

773,000 words. The Koran is divided into 114 surahs in 30 volumes. The New Testament is divided into 27 books, 260 chapters, and 7,956 verses.

Those who have studied literature will better remember Shakespeare's thirty-seven plays by dividing them into three categories: comedy, history, and tragedy. If you'd like to remember the countries in Europe, it's easier to learn them by region: Scandinavia, Western Europe, Eastern Europe, the Mediterranean countries.

It's much easier to remember a grocery list by breaking it up into groups. For instance, take the following sample list: milk, yogurt, chicken breasts, tomatoes, butter, hamburgers, peppers, and carrots. Odds are you won't remember such a list if the items on it have no connection. For this reason, I recommend dividing the above eight items into three categories with a common denominator:

> "**G**o buy a loaf of bread and some milk," Esther tells her husband, Morris. "That's two items. Please remember."
>
> When Morris returns home after three hours, Esther opens the shopping bag, and sure enough she finds two items—a can of sardines and a dozen eggs.
>
> "What am I going to do with you, Mo? Can't you remember two simple items?" she sighs. "I said tomatoes and apple juice! What's so difficult about that?"

Dairy products: milk, yogurt, butter (three items)
Vegetables: tomatoes, peppers, carrots (three items)
Meat: chicken breasts, hamburgers (two items)

(Personally, I never need shopping lists—not because I use memory techniques, but simply because I throw everything I want into the shopping cart.)

USE CATEGORIES

As a fast solution to remembering something, try organizing the required information into groups. In a figurative way, it's easier to eat a spoonful of peas than one pea at a time.

A sequence of numbers—say, 4, 6, 5, 2, 3, 3, 7, 4, 7—is easier to recall if it's divided into groups. In this case, you could think of it as 465-233-747. The numbers 747 will be even easier to recall if they're associated with a Boeing 747.

Look what   happens to the brain   when   patterns suddenly change. When   words are   suddenly spaced   farther   away from   each other, so   that   each   word   stands more onitsown,   the   brain suddenly has   to   stop   instead of flow along   with the   words.   . I know, this is   getting   irritating.I've   made   my   point. Let's go back to normal.

USE ABBREVIATIONS AND ACRONYMS

Abbreviations make reading and writing more convenient, plus they're helpful memory aids.

We all use the abbreviations B.C. (before Christ) and A.D. (Anno Domini) in relation to time. Most people know what the NYPD is, even if they don't live in New York City or have any dealings with its police department. In everyday communication we use abbreviations without even being aware of it: DNA (deoxyribonucleic acid), PIN (personal identification number), and so on. Sometimes acronyms are used as shortcuts in texts.

This method was founded as the result of an archaeological

expedition in the Judean desert in Israel. Coins from the Bar Kochba rebellion against the Romans during the years A.D. 132–135 were found with the Hebrew letters Sha B L'HaR imprinted on them—*Sh*anah (year), *B* (two) *L'HeR*ut (of freedom).

> A man enters a pharmacy and asks the pharmacist, "Can you please give me some tablets of acetylsalicylic acid?"
>
> "You mean aspirin," the pharmacist replies.
>
> "Right—I just never manage to remember that name."

Think how different the study of chemistry would be without an abbreviation system. The compound $C_{18}H_{30}$ is also known as dodecylbenzene. What name would you prefer to memorize?

Here's an example from your typical daily to-do list: What needs to be done before you leave your home in the morning. For example:

1. Take your *wallet*.
2. Turn off the *stove*.
3. Lock the *door*.

Remember WSL (pronounce it like *whistle*) as the initials for *wallet*, *stove*, and *lock*. And so, every morning, "whistle" as you leave the house (that is, WSL), not just to get your day off to a positive start, but to help you recall what needs to be done.

ACROSTICS AND REVERSE ACRONYMS ("BACKRONYMS")

Psalm 119 is a terrific example of acrostics that aid the memory. Verses 1–8 each have a first word beginning with the Hebrew letter aleph, verses 9–16 each have a first word beginning with the Hebrew letter bet, and so on.

A group of words can also be reduced to a single acronym. Using this method in reverse—what some call "backronyms"—can help you remember complex passwords, such as those for your online bank account, e-mail account, combination lock, or the launch of a nuclear missile.

Let's say you're the owner of an Irish ice cream parlor, when suddenly you spot a group of salesmen approaching, hoping to sell you kosher popsicles. Frantically, you instruct one of your employees, Brian McNuggetosh, to quickly turn off the lights and lock the doors. The password for your state-of-the-art electronic lock system is PMBJ3K5, but there's no chance that McNuggetosh is going to remember this, because he's panicking. If he knew the following trick, though, it wouldn't be a problem.

Think of the password as an acronym for a sentence of some kind. Each letter in the password is the first letter of some word. For example, PMBJ3K5 can be turned into the sentence "**P**lease **m**ake **b**ig **J**ohn **3** shots of **K5**" (which is some kind of cocktail our beefy friend John likes). Nice, right? This trick transforms something entirely nonsensical into something that you and McNuggetosh can remember effortlessly.

Use "backronyms" to remember complicated codes and passwords . . . or, heck, just write 'em down on a Post-it note, stick it on your PC, and get it over with.

Backronyms are also useful as mnemonic devices for learning. Say you're studying biology. Remembering the sentence "King Philip could only find three green socks" will assist you in remembering the order of taxonomy: kingdom, phylum, class, order, family, genus, species.

In my Super Student Success seminars, students come up with great acronyms. Here are some ideas that were brought up in a recent seminar in Singapore:

$E = MC^2$ (the mass/energy equivalence)
Einstein **m**akes **c**omplicated **square**s

$ax^2 + bx + c = 0$ (the quadratic equation)
A **square axe** hits a **box** and cancels it—thus, it **equals** 0

H_2O (water)
Hard **to** **ob**tain

Backronyms have other wonderful uses, but we'll keep them a surprise for later.

Meanwhile, here are some humorous ones:

El Al (Israel's national airline)
Every landing always late . . . or Every luggage always lost

TWA
Try with another

Fiat (Italian car)
Fix it again, Tony

FUN WITH ZIGZAGS: THE JEWISH SYSTEM OF PARALLEL ACRONYMS

McNuggentosh could also benefit from learning an interesting Jewish way to remember measurements and monetary units, used also in ancient times.

During the Mishnaic era, sometime around 70–190 CE, the local currency in the Holy Land was issued in the form of six coins: sela, dinar, me'ah, pondyon, isair, and pruta. Now, how did they remember how many dinars were in a sela, and how many me'ahs in a dinar? They created acronyms using the first letter of each coin—SaDaM PIP—and grouped them with the acronym DOBeBaH. Take a look at this before you get too nervous:

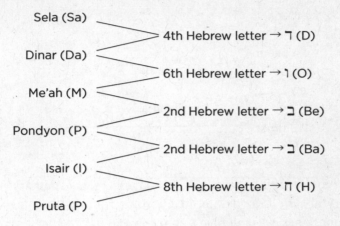

As you can see, using this method makes it easy to remember that a sela has *D*, or four dinars; that O me'ahs, meaning six me'ahs, equal one dinar; and so on. (If Morris and Esther lived in ancient times, I could envisage Morris with the sardines and eggs at the checkout counter in the quick mart. "Excuse me, sir," he'd say to the cashier. "Do you accept selas, or would you prefer that I pay in pondyons?")

Let's say you want to remember the structure of a company in Napoleon's army. Each company contains 140 soldiers: 1 captain, 1 farrier, 2 lieutenants, 5 sergeants, 8 corporals, 3 drummers, and the rest privates. Let's create acronyms using the first letter of each position—*CaFe*(u) *LieSeCoD* (captain, farrier, lieutenant, sergeant, corporal, drummer)—grouping them with an acronym for the numbers, AA BE HiC, where A = 1, B = 2, E = 5, H = 8, and C = 3:

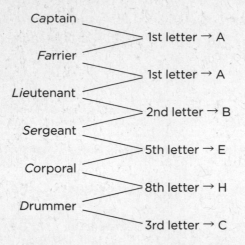

Now imagine that you are studying French military history in Cafe Liesecod, located not far from the Bastille. You want to get AA (a double A in the exam) in order to BE HiC! ("What's *hic*?" you may ask. You'll have to figure that out for yourself.) Complicated and illogical as this system may seem, you'll be surprised to find out how well it works once you try it.

So take a shot at it. Use parallel zigzags or backronyms to remember the units in the metric system: kilometer, hectometer, dekameter, meter, decimeter, centimeter, millimeter.

We've covered quite a bit of ground thus far. Let's quickly review the basic principles needed for a masterful memory:

1. *Trust* your memory to serve you well.
2. Find the *motivation* to improve your memory in the areas which you deem weak.
3. *Pay attention* to details, people, and anything else you want to remember.
4. Find *interest* in the things you wish to remember.

5. Create *associative* connections using guided imagery.
6. *Organize* and process new information in a way you'll easily access in the future.

The better we know how to file information in the correct location in our memory (such as facts, reports, and documents), the better we will be able to retrieve it when we need to.

CHAPTER 8

~~~~~~~~~~~~~~~~~

ANCIENT MENTAL FILING SYSTEMS

EVEN THROUGH THE darkest periods in history, there have been those who have strived to make the world a better place. While politicians and military leaders wielded their influence and power, notables like Socrates, Plato, Cicero, Jesus, and Rabbi Akiva—among many others—sought to enhance human intellect and develop methods to help the human mind.

During the Roman period, some of the most practical and noteworthy memory techniques were born. Why then? I'll refer once again to the magical word in this book— *motivation*. Take Cicero, for example—one of the greatest orators the world has ever known. What would have been his motivation to develop a super memory? Let's see . . .

Cicero is sitting beneath a pine tree, preparing a speech and contemplating. "Okay," he thinks. "There are two thousand people waiting to hear me speak at Madison Square

Coliseum and I need to talk for three hours. Hmm . . . I could use PowerPoint for a stunning presentation. Oh, wait, they haven't invented that yet. How about an overhead projector? Nope; that doesn't exist either. Perhaps I'll just rev up the DVD . . . video . . . slide projector . . . Yikes! I guess I'll just have to develop a great memory instead." And he did.

As did others, who understood that an advanced human memory is more affordable—and more efficient—than the most advanced technology.

THE ROMAN ROOM METHOD

We've already learned the basic principle of creating associative links. We've seen how a succession of absurd images connected to one another is easy to remember. However, the associative link method cannot stand on its own. The trick is to create "hooks" or "hangers" as the base for the most effective use of memory.

I compare this to a closet which houses dozens of hangers. On each hanger hangs a garment: on one a blouse, on another a pair of trousers, on the next one a jacket, and then there's a hanger with a shirt. The garments may change, but the hangers remain fixed. It's the same with information we want to remember. The information may vary; however, the "hooks" in our memory on which we "hang" the information should remain constant.

Confused? Don't be. In order to show you how this works, let's look at the difference between short-term and long-term memory.

Short-term memory lasts from a few seconds up to several minutes. When we call information to get a phone

> "Right now I'm having amnesia and déjà vu at the same time. I think I've forgotten this before."
> —STEVEN WRIGHT

number, most of us mumble it quickly to ourselves, hoping to remember it for as long as it takes to dial the number. If there is no answer or the line is busy, we may end up calling information again, frustrated and embarrassed. It turns out that our short-term memory is very short indeed!

Most of the new information our mind absorbs is stored in our short-term memory. Yet when someone says something that makes a great impression on us, it will immediately be stored in our long-term memory. This information will remain there forever, and we'll be able to retrieve it at any time.

When we talk about developing an excellent memory, we actually mean the transfer of information from our short-term memory to our long-term memory. Long-term memory is like an information bank in which we deposit all we know. The information is safely stored in the bank. We cannot lose it since it isn't possible to forget it.

> Queen Elizabeth I of England once got into a quarrel with a certain man who, in turn, was sent to exile in America. Thirty years later, he returned to the kingdom. He presented himself to the queen and asked her if she remembered him.
>
> "No," the queen answered decisively. "I specifically remember that I had forgotten you."

Just try to forget your name. Inconceivable! This information has been stored in your long-term memory since a very young age and remains engraved there forever (excluding abnormal memory loss due to illness or physical damage).

Some things are simply unforgettable. Our goal is to use unforgettable information as a fixed hook on which we hang short-term information. In other words, we will take new information we want to remember and tie it to pieces of information that we cannot forget.

So how does this work? I won't keep you in suspense.

Actually, I will.

First, a short, tragic story—with a cool ending.

Many years ago, a Greek poet called Simonides lived by the Aegean Sea. One evening, he was invited to a dinner party at a wealthy friend's home. During the lavish meal, Simonides was called to come outside. While Simonides and the man who had summoned him were engaging in conversation, an earthquake struck. The house in which Simonides had been sitting only a few minutes previously collapsed, burying underneath it all the dinner guests.

After clearing out the rubble, the village residents had a difficult time identifying the deceased guests. The only one able to help was Simonides, who could recall the order in which each guest was seated around the dinner table. He remembered each one by visualizing them around the table, taking note of their exact location.

"He inferred that persons desiring to train this faculty [memory] must select places and form mental images of the things they wish to remember and store those images in the places, so that the order of the places will preserve the order of the things, and the images of the things will denote the things themselves," explains Cicero in *De Oratore*. In later years, the Romans perfected the "memory according to location" technique. It is now referred to as the "method of loci."

A more current example is our ability to remember the structure and contents of our home. We know exactly what our living room looks like, right? We remember where our couch and television are located. We know what's to the left and to the right of the TV, and so on. All we have to do is to tie new information to these items.

Marcus Tullius Cicero, the great Roman orator, not only wrote about this method but was an avid user of it in his fervent speeches. Cicero stood in front of his fellow country-men and spoke passionately about every topic in the world—all from memory. It must have been very impressive to observe him speaking so confidently without the need for notes. How did Cicero achieve this? He planned his speeches according to the "Roman room method." He imagined his home and attached the topics of his speech to the items in his home.

Let's imagine Cicero's home for a moment:

- At the entrance to the house is a gate with two pillars.
- Inside the entrance is a hallway with a sculpture of a Roman goddess perched in the center.
- In the living room sits a three-seat sofa.
- The kitchen is to the left of the living room.
- Near the kitchen, a stairway leads up to the second floor.
- Upstairs there is a bedroom with a canopied king-size bed.

Now, let's imagine what Cicero plans to speak on:

- The appointment of two new ministers.
- The new army's uniforms, designed by fashion guru Georgius Armanius.
- The upcoming annual civil guard lineup (emphasizing sharpened arrows, state-of-the-art armor, and polished sandals).
- The newly instituted "Maintain Your Horse" campaign.
- The local sport championships scheduled for next month.
- The yearly vacation for the bureaucrats who excelled in their work at the educational facility near Capri.

Now all he has to do is tie these issues to the structure and contents of his home:

- At the gate, near the *two pillars*, he imagines his *two new ministers* each hugging and kissing a pillar.
- He envisions the *Roman goddess sculpture* decked out in the army's *new uniform* (poor thing was naked).
- On the *three-seat sofa*, he sees a *sharpened arrow* embedded in the first seat's upholstery, *shining armor* tied to the second seat, and *polished sandals* resting on the third seat.
- Inside the *kitchen*, he pictures a *horse* munching on hay scattered all over the floor.
- Dozens of *athletes* run up and down the *staircase*.
- And on his *bed*, he sees a fat civil servant snoozing away. On the medal hanging from a ribbon around his neck is engraved *Capri or Bust—Top Bureaucrat of 22 B.C.*

On the day of the weekly lineup, Cicero stands in front of his audience. Now he starts his virtual tour of his home.

He first thinks about the entrance gate and the two pillars. What does he remember about those pillars? Yep, the two new ministers.

Inside his house, the Roman goddess sculpture looks quite amusing. Cicero immediately remembers why, and starts talking about Georgius Armanius's new uniforms.

In his living room, what does he see? Three things: a sharpened arrow, standardized armor, and polished sandals.

Then Cicero turns to his left. What does he see there? A horse. In florid Latin, Cicero explains the "Maintain Your Horse" campaign, emphasizing the importance of keeping one's horse healthy in the winter. Certainly masses of horses with colds and runny noses would be a disgrace to the Roman emperor.

Continuing his imaginary home tour, Cicero intends to go upstairs to his beautiful bedroom, but he can't. Dozens of athletes get in his way as they run up and down the stairs. "Local sport championships next month," Cicero enthusiastically shares with his audience.

Cicero does make it to his bedroom and envisions the bureaucrat napping comfortably in his warm bed. He immediately remembers that the man has earned such peace and quiet. "Vacation in Capri for exemplary civil servants," he shares with the crowd. He knew this was the way to end his speech. Two hundred geeky Romans become instantly motivated by the enticing thought of a golden beach, a blue ocean, and Byzantine tourists in bikinis.

Two thousand years have passed since then, and nothing has changed—the human memory today is no different, and the techniques used then are just as relevant. The only difference is proficiency. The Romans considered the memory an important asset. Therefore, the Romans obsessively worked on developing techniques and implementing them in their daily lives.

Today, we are very far from the skills they had mastered way back then. The Romans weren't more gifted—they were just better trained. In the coming chapters, we too will learn to develop this proficiency.

But first, let's return to today and look at our own home.

To us, our home is the most intimate place in the universe. As it's a place we know so well, everything associated with it is stored in our long-term memory. We designed it; we invested in it; we decided what goes inside and where it belongs.

A doctor told an anxious woman that there was no hope for her poor husband and they would have to disconnect the life support machine and stop all fluids. So one day, while he was sitting on the couch in the living room, she cut the TV cable and threw away all the beer cans.

We spend a great amount of our time at home. Our home is where some of our family members wait impatiently for others to return the car . . .

Let's start by creating a list of "hooks"—reference points in our home—just as Cicero did, so find some paper and a pen. Then choose four rooms in your house (for example, the living room, bedroom, kitchen, and bathroom). Imagine yourself entering these rooms, and write down five items you see in each room. It's important that you write down these items according to their placement in the room.

Also, it's important that you choose the rooms in the order they are situated in your home. For instance, in my house, just to the left of the entrance hall is the kitchen. So then, the kitchen will be room #1. After this, I imagine walking to the other rooms after the kitchen. Next is the living room (room #2), my bedroom (room #3), and the bathroom (room #4).

After choosing your four rooms, go into the first room and select five pieces of furniture or fixtures. It's best to choose larger items. These items should be different from one another (for instance, don't choose two chairs). As mentioned, it's important that the items chosen be in the order you see them—clockwise or counterclockwise from the room's entrance. Under no circumstances should you jump from one item to another randomly. Write down the items you have in your kitchen, from one to five, in their order. My kitchen, for instance, consists of the following items: refrigerator, sink, microwave, stove, and an original Rembrandt painting (at least that's what the guy at the flea market told me).

Afterward, mentally walk into the other rooms and do the very same. Don't repeat items you have already chosen. For example, don't choose the dining room table if you already chose the kitchen table.

After you are done, you should have a list consisting of twenty items. Here is an example of a list:

Room #1 (Kitchen)
1. Refrigerator
2. Sink
3. Microwave
4. Stove
5. Table

Room #2 (Living Room)
6. Stereo system
7. Television
8. Bookshelf
9. Couch
10. Lamp

Room #3 (Bedroom)
11. Closet
12. Mirror
13. Dresser
14. Bed
15. Life-size poster of Angelina Jolie

Room #4 (Bathroom)
16. Shower
17. Bathtub
18. Towel rack
19. Toilet
20. Laundry basket

This list is an essential base for everything we will get to later on. For this reason, it's highly important that it becomes imprinted in your memory. You should be able to recite it even if suddenly awakened in the middle of the night. You should know it by heart, and be able to extract it from your memory at the same speed you remember your telephone number or your name—in a split second!

Now we'll work on this list until it's firmly implanted in our minds.

First, go over it again and make sure no items are duplicated. Make sure that they are indeed listed in the order they are placed in the room. For example, if in room #2 the couch is placed after the stereo system and TV, while the bookshelf is on the parallel wall, the couch should be item #8 and the bookshelf item #9.

It's time to practice, so let's perform the following steps:

1. Read the first item on the list. Say it out loud. If you wish, close your eyes and imagine the item in detail. If it's a refrigerator, imagine its color. Try to remember its height and its brand name; listen to the noise of its compressor. Do the same with the second item, the third, and so on. Take ten minutes to do this now.

2. Go over the list a second time. Do this right away—don't allow yourself any breaks right now. Make sure that each item's image is crystal clear. Do not try to remember the order of the items; just read the list of items from your sheet of paper.

3. Repeat the previous exercise, only this time begin with the last item (#20) and review it in reverse order.

4. Next, do this a little faster. Whisper the first item, then shut your eyes and picture it. Open your eyes, whisper the second item, then shut your eyes and envision the second item. Continue doing so with the rest of your list.

5. Now put the paper aside. It's time to start the imaginary tour of your house. Go to room #1, and look inside the room. Imagine the first item and say out loud what it is. Continue clockwise (or counterclockwise) and get to the second item. Say what it is and envision it clearly.

6. Let's do this once more. However, this time we'll begin from the bottom of the list and move up to the top. Imagine entering room #4 and envision the last item in it; say its name out loud. Now, name the nineteenth item on the list, then the eighteenth, and so on up to the first item.

7. Do it again, a little faster. Begin with the first item and go over the rest one by one. Review the items as if they were on a production line. You don't have to name them out loud. You should be able to do this more quickly now.

8. Repeat once more, going even faster. According to my assessment, at this stage you should have the ability to go over the list in a matter of seconds!

This organized, itemized list is the first step toward enabling you to remember various memory tasks, including tremendous amounts of study material, in half the time it would take you to study the traditional way.

THE NUMBER-PICTURE SYSTEM

The Jews were aware of the Roman room method; Rabbi Leon (Yehuda Aryeh) of Modena mentions this system in his work *Lev HaAryeh* (Lion heart). I guess Jewish scholars thought this system had great potential . . . if only they had a permanent home! As a wandering people who needed to think fast and act quickly, they came up with their own memorizing system. While the Romans remembered their homes by heart, the Jews preferred letters and numbers. You can't forget the alphabet, can you? And if you know how to count to 10, you're set.

Instead of struggling to imagine the number 1, Rabbi Aryeh suggested imagining a spear or a lance because it physically resembles the shape of the number 1.

Instead of the number 2, he suggested imagining Noah's ark because the animals came in pairs.

Does the number 3 resemble anything to you? Well, the rabbi was probably eating his dinner when he realized that the number 3 looks like a fork.

Let's say the number 4 is a saw. Imagine yourself holding the 4's leg, and begin to saw back and forth.

The number 5 is most closely associated with the shape of a hand consisting of five fingers, unless you've lost one after unsuccessfully using the previous number (the saw). In the Arab world, the *hamsa* (a decorative hand figure) is a common symbol against the evil eye and even

earthquakes, and today, many Jewish homes are adorned with hamsas on the walls to scare away bad spirits, bad luck, and Good Samaritans knocking on doors and asking for donations.

To picture the number 6, think about Captain Hook, who perhaps had a hard time visualizing the number 5 after losing his own hand to the wrath of a crocodile. Number 6 actually looks like a large hook that is bent into a loop at one end.

Let's keep going. What can we associate the number 7 with? Seven days in a week. Imagine a weekly planner as a visual for the number 7.

Number 8 is easy—it looks just like a pair of eyeglasses.

What about number 9? A woman is pregnant for nine months, so 9 will be an expectant woman.

And finally . . . number 10.

I'd associate number 10 with Bo Derek and the movie that made her (and her hair) famous, but that would *not* be Rabbi Aryeh's association. I'm guessing he'd go with the Ten Commandments.

Now that we're familiar with the number-picture system, how can we put it into practice? Let's say you need to remember to buy a few things for your office or class. Your list includes green and yellow highlighters, a folder, and some Wite-Out. The idea is like Cicero with the Roman room method—you simply utilize one of your additional mental filing cabinets.

Think of your office or home. The drawers are most efficiently organized in a numerical or alphabetical way, right? Open up the first drawer (symbolized by a spear) and create an absurd association between **highlighters** and a **spear**. Imagine throwing a magical highlighting spear at a distant document—when the spear strikes, all the main points are highlighted.

Then open your second drawer, which is represented by **Noah's ark**. Imagine the ark filled with thousands of **folders** scattered about. The animals might as well do some paperwork instead of being bored for forty days at sea. However, the ark is so messy with the scattered folders that there's no place to walk.

The third drawer is a **fork**. The third thing you wanted to buy was **Wite-Out**. What kind of connection can you make between a fork and correction fluid? Imagine a fork coated with Wite-Out. Every time you put the fork in your mouth, some Wite-Out remains on your lips, and you end up needing to wipe off the Wite-Out. Of course, this doesn't need to be the association you would have chosen by yourself. What's so great about this system is that you can create the associations most relevant to yourself.

The next time you walk into an office supply store, stand there for a moment and think, "What the heck do I need to buy today?" Then open up your mental file cabinet, just as you'd open a notebook or journal or glance at a note you'd written to yourself. The first drawer is represented by a picture of a spear. What image did we connect to the spear? The highlighting markers. Walk over to the shelf with the markers and choose your highlighters. By the way, what colors are you looking for? I'm sure you remember.

The next one is Noah's ark. What was scattered in the ark? "Those messy animals. I'll have to buy new folders. . . ."

Then comes a fork. The fork was coated with peanut butter, right? (Just giving you a hard time. I'm sure you clearly remember the Wite-Out.)

Here is a quick review of the number-picture system:

The Number-Picture System

1	Spear	6	Hook
2	Noah's ark	7	Weekly planner
3	Fork	8	Pair of eyeglasses
4	Saw	9	Pregnant woman
5	Hand	10	Ten Commandments

When you wake up tomorrow morning, give this mental filing system a try and jump-start a refreshingly efficient day.

PART III

USE IT
OR
LOSE IT:
HOW TO REMEMBER
PRACTICALLY
ANYTHING

MAYBE
YOU'LL REMEMBER
TO VISIT YOUR MOTHER
ONCE IN A WHILE—
SHE SHOULD BE SO LUCKY.

CHAPTER 9

MISSION ACCOMPLISHED: PAPERS, DUTIES, AND TASK BUSTERS

Patient: "Doctor, I can't remember anything. What do you suggest I do?"

Doctor: "Pay me now."

I ONCE SAW an amusing list posted on an office wall entitled "The Ten Commandments for Tired People." Perhaps you can identify with some of the "commandments":

"I was born tired, and resting is my mission in life."
"If work means health, suggest it to the sick."
"If you feel like working, sit down for a minute, and the feeling shall pass."

And then there was the one that we *all* can relate to: "Don't put off for tomorrow what you can put off for the day after."

Is there anyone among us who doesn't procrastinate? "No problem, this can wait till tomorrow," we reassure ourselves. "Next week I'll be in the city anyway, so I'll visit Aunt Mary then." "I really don't feel like going to the post office—I can mail in that traffic fine some other time."

The days pass, and the days become weeks. Then sometime in the middle of September, we realize—to our great dismay—that we never did pay that fine. Yep, the one that was due April 3.

We suddenly remember that we never paid back the $50 our friend Sharon loaned us. And that's really unpleasant, because we borrowed the cash two months ago. We really did mean to pay her back.

Oh, man—the final date to turn in the term paper is this Thursday. Oh well, we'll have to ask for an extension . . . again.

We all need to work on this human shortcoming. In this book, we'll focus on those tasks that really do slip our minds, and maybe we'll find that procrastination is less of an issue for us.

Let's begin by planning tomorrow. Here's a list of tasks you might want to remember to accomplish.

Things to Do Tomorrow

1. Return the DVD to the movie rental place.
2. Pay back Sharon the $50 I borrowed from her.
3. Draw up my personal sales report.
4. Go to the post office: pay for that traffic ticket and buy twenty stamps.
5. Send flowers for Monica's birthday.

Each one of us has a system for remembering daily chores. Most people opt for a notepad, a calendar, BlackBerry, or

Post-it note. The use of memory techniques is not intended to replace the notepad or any of these other tools. The techniques are intended to help us out in those instances when the notepad isn't available. The most worthwhile reason to use memory techniques is the typical phenomenon which I like to call the "sudden must-remember attack." I'm talking about the cases in which we remember something important while we're doing something else. Usually what we're doing won't allow us to deal with the task, or even write it down so that we can take care of it later. We'll deal with both—remembering tasks without needing physical reminders, and learning how to remember to do them at the exact time they really need to be done.

Say you're driving, and suddenly you remember that Rachel called you this morning. You promised to call her back (which you didn't) and your cell phone's battery is now dead. "Can't do it now but *must* remember this for later," you tell yourself.

You're talking with a client, when all of a sudden you remember that you have to ship out an order to one of your reps.

You're on the elevator early one evening and start thinking about David. You recall that you promised him an answer regarding the concert tonight, and it's already seven o'clock.

In these scenarios, a notepad will be of no use. It won't help remind you to call Rachel after you charge your phone, for example.

With this reality in mind, we need to learn how to link our to-do tasks to one of our mental reminders—say, our room or our drawers (the number-picture system)—and store them in our long-term memory.

FILING IN OUR MENTAL MEMORY CABINET:
IMPLEMENTING THE ROMAN ROOM METHOD

Remember the list we made up of the items in our home, and how Cicero used a similar list to help jog his memory for his famous speeches to the masses?

What do you do with your phone bills, insurance policies, bank statements, etc.? You probably stash them away in different files, right? Some of the files you may have in your cabinet include "household expenditures," "bank," and "car." This is exactly the way we will organize new information in the "files" of our memory. We will be able to access them using our imagination anytime we choose.

For example, one mental file—say, the kitchen—will contain tomorrow's to-do list. Another mental file—the living room—will house the "phone calls to return" list. Another file, the bedroom: "Cute boys to invite for the New Year's Eve party." This is how it works. We'll start by filing the to-do list in the "kitchen." As we learned, the aim is to link the existing items—the ones at home—to the new items, the things we have to do tomorrow.

1. We'll imagine the item on our home list as vividly as we can.
2. We'll take what needs to be done and turn it into a distinct image.
3. We'll tie the two together in the most absurd, ridiculous, and unconventional manner.

Take the first item on our kitchen list—the refrigerator. Our first task is to return the DVD we rented, so let's link the two together.

Imagine that we open the refrigerator door and see dozens of DVDs neatly organized on the different shelves and in the compartments. On one shelf we have science fiction; visualize the sci-fi label on every DVD cover. The dairy compartment contains dramas (the "milkier" movies). The meat compartment is full of action movies.

The second item on our kitchen list is the sink. The second task on tomorrow's to-do list is pay back Sharon her $50. We'll create an associative link between Sharon's $50 and the sink. We may imagine Sharon standing by our sink with the water running, happily washing a $50 bill. First she scrubs it with the sponge. Then she rinses off the soap with warm water. At last she waves the bill in the air in order to dry it. Throughout this money-laundering procedure, she's looking toward us and smiling, as if to say, "Don't forget my money, honey."

The third item on our kitchen list is the microwave oven. The next thing we need to remember to do is draw up our personal sales report. Open the microwave oven door in your mind. Put a stack of clean white paper inside, shut the door, and program the oven for five minutes, on high. Watch as the stack of paper twirls on the glass microwave tray. Notice how the papers begin to turn golden, and slowly letters and then words appear on them. When five minutes are up, the microwave beeps. Remove a detailed written report, which is even bound and covered for presentation. (Wouldn't it be wonderful to have such an intelligent microwave oven?)

The fourth item on our kitchen list is the stove. The fourth task we must remember to do tomorrow is go to the post office. We have two things we need to do there: pay that parking ticket, and buy twenty stamps so we can send bills to people who actually owe us money. Let's imagine that a huge parking ticket, the size of a billboard, is attached to the stove. On it, the fine amount is boldly imprinted on it in bright red.

All our efforts to get this ticket off the stove are in vain. We're only able to remove tiny bits of paper, while most of the ticket remains. On one burner, we're boiling up twenty stamps in a saucepan. Every so often, we'll stir the stamps using a large wooden spoon. The stamps are now "cooked" and ready to be secured onto the envelopes.

We finally get to the last item on today's kitchen list—the table. Our last task for tomorrow is to send flowers to Monica for her birthday. Envision your kitchen table clearly, and imagine you have magically turned it into a huge garden. It's covered with soil and dozens of red roses grow from it. In the middle sits a huge birthday card with "Happy Birthday, Monica!" written across the cover.

The same rules we used to connect items in the previous chapters apply here as well. You must envision the pictures sharply and clearly, and use exaggerated and absurd images. For instance, if you find one of the scenes you envisioned ends up being boring, it isn't an effective association. You won't be able to remember something that bores you. Weird, ridiculous, and illogical pictures are easy to remember because they're simply more interesting.

In order to create a sharper, clearer image, guide yourself by asking questions about the images: "What is Sharon wearing while she's washing the cash?" "What pictures are on the stamps I'm cooking?" "When I took the report out of the microwave oven, did it smell like microwave popcorn?"

IT'S TOMORROW. WHERE'S YOUR TO-DO LIST?

Good morning. You've already had breakfast and brushed your teeth, and you're about to leave the house. Now is the perfect time to take out the "things to do today" file and put it to use. Remember where you kept it? Right—in the kitchen. Pull out the kitchen index from your memory and sort through the dividers (meaning the items).

The first item is the refrigerator. Open the refrigerator door. What do you see in there? DVDs arranged neatly on the shelves. "Wow, it's good that I haven't left the house yet," you mutter. You head over to the coffee table and put the DVD into your bag.

Now continue your virtual tour of the kitchen. Going clockwise (or counterclockwise, your choice), you quickly turn to the second item, the sink. What have you connected to the kitchen sink? Sharon and the $50 you owe her, right?

The third item is the microwave oven. What did you heat up in it? Say this out loud: "My personal sales report."

What's the fourth item? The stove. And what does the stove remind you of? The ticket that is attached to it and the stamps you have to buy. This will remind you that you have to go to the post office.

Now you get to the fifth and final item: the kitchen table. What does it remind you of? The flowers you want to send Monica for her birthday.

Now that you've reviewed today's to-do list, you can leave the house relaxed, knowing exactly what needs to be done.

"Relaxed?" you retort. "Wait a minute. There are two things that bother me a bit. Number one, how will I remember to go over the list in the morning and during the day? Number two, the fact that I remembered to return money to Sharon doesn't guarantee that I'll remember to give it to her when I see her!"

Regarding the first question, I'll take the political approach and answer with a question of my own. How do you remember to check your calendar throughout the day? You make a habit of it. I suggest that you open your virtual calendar regularly as well. This way you'll become accustomed to going over important mental files several times a day, and at set times.

For the answer to the second question, there's a fun solution.

THE "ONLINE" REMINDER SYSTEM

So you've got this list of things you need to do. And as we all know, this list is mainly a declaration of intention. In reality, things change. We find that tasks get put off or slip our mind because we were busy doing something else. While you did indeed place the DVD movie in your bag, the problem is that you forgot to stop at the movie rental store when you drove by it. And though you did run into Sharon and it was really nice to see her, you again forgot to give her the money you owe her.

In the world of computers, there is software to correct problems as they occur. In most word processing software, text is saved automatically even if you fail to manually save it every so often. Airplanes have software installed to warn the pilot of any irregularities, such as if the plane is positioned at a dangerous angle or the fuel is running low.

What about us? We are, indeed, quite advanced human machines. The problem is that we have only a hard disk—meaning, we have only one head with one memory system. We cannot open the A drive or the B drive. We cannot put in a disk and solve problems using external software. The responsibility for "programming" is on us. We'll be able to remember only if we decide that we really do want to remember, and program our memory to carry out certain actions at a certain time.

In order to remember to perform a task or an action at a certain time and in a particular situation, we need to create an associative link between the place, situation, and action.

Back to repaying Sharon that $50. It may be that she works

with you and her office is on the fourth floor, while yours is on the second. If so, visualize walking from the parking lot to the building's entrance when you arrive at work in the morning. See the entrance door. Open the door and walk to the elevator. Press the Up button. Inside the elevator, imagine that you're going to the fourth floor instead of the second. Think about this scenario several times, and you'll find that when you enter the elevator tomorrow, you'll feel a bit funny about pressing the button for the second floor. Although you press it every morning, your heightened awareness will bring you to realize that today's the day you should press the button for the fourth floor.

- In case Sharon doesn't work with you, imagine a different scenario. Since you owe her money, you are not allowed to hug or kiss her when you see her this time. Imagine her approaching you with a smile, but right before the hug or kiss, you pull back. This embarrassing situation is imagined, of course; when you really do see her, you won't do this. However, that strange feeling will remind you that you need to pay her back.

Say you've decided to go to the post office during your lunch break. It's right next to the restaurant where you plan to dine. Imagine that when you get into your car you've got a flat tire, courtesy of angry cops out to punish you for not paying your traffic fine. When you actually do get into your car at lunchtime to head to the restaurant, you'll sense something wrong with your car. This "off" feeling will remind you of the flat tire you imagined, and in turn, the flat tire will remind you of the ticket you still need to pay.

In order to remember to send Monica her birthday flowers, try any one of the following ideas. My top choice would

> A cop once pulled over a Hells Angel who was riding his Harley-Davidson at an excessive speed.
>
> "What exactly am I supposed to do with this?" the motorcyclist sneered when the cop handed him the speeding ticket.
>
> "Ah, it's quite simple," the cop answered. "Collect three of these and you get a bicycle."

be that right after you finish reviewing your to-do list, which is now filed in your memory, you call the florist and give him Monica's address.

"What?" I hear you exclaiming. "Immediately? First thing in the morning? Can't I put this off until I've checked my e-mail and had four cups of coffee?" Yes, we are talking about an extreme solution, so if you just can't swallow it, I'll offer a more palatable suggestion. Visualize your office. Imagine that as you arrive at the office, there's a flower arrangement covering your computer monitor. You even "see" green leaves growing out of your phone. When you get to the office (in reality), you'll sense that something is missing. Ah, yes—flowers and foliage, which are really meant for Monica. Better call the florist now before you forget.

For those of you who still aren't convinced this method will work, I agree with you. If you don't think it will, it won't.

For those of you who are (I hope) excited about using the "online" reminder system, or, at least, are willing to give it a try, to you—I promise success. I have no other way of convincing you that this method works; you'll have to try it for yourself.

I'll repeat myself once more: the images you conjure up in your imagination *must* be clear. Pressing the button for the fourth floor or seeing leaves growing from the phone *must* elicit a clear, sharp, and strong picture. If the picture is fuzzy, the necessary associative link will not be strong, and you won't be reminded to carry out the task at hand.

THE 911 METHOD

It's unavoidable—the dreaded sudden must-remember attack. What do you do when it strikes? Like when you need to return a call but your cell phone battery is dead? Or when it dawns on you right in the thick of a conversation with a new client that you need to get an order shipped ASAP?

Drumroll, please . . . the mental filing method comes to our rescue. If we use the kitchen as a file for tomorrow's to-do list, let's open a new mental file for the sudden must-remember list.

Pick another room from your room list—the living room, for example. We'll decide that the living room will be used to file those suddenly remembered tasks. So when you're driving home from work and you suddenly remember that you have to call Suzie, no problem. Mentally open your living room file. Take out the first item on the list, the stereo system. Make a quick link between Suzie and the stereo system. You may opt to imagine her jumping on it, inflicting great damage. This will really upset you, because you forked out big bucks for it.

You're talking with a client when you remember you have to ship out an important order. While listening to her, and without her knowing, bring out the second item from your living room list—the television. Quickly imagine that the person waiting for the order is being interviewed by Jay Leno.

Did it just hit you that you never gave David an answer about the concert? Head over to your mental bookshelf, the third item on the living room list. Imagine David trying to climb on top of it. Envision the shelves caving in and all of the books crashing to the floor, along with David.

Later on you can go over the kitchen list. Then you'll add the living room list, and rejoice over how easily you remembered everything! No need to continue to frustrate yourself as you try to recall all those things you wanted to do but couldn't do right then and there. No longer will you wonder, "What did I remember that needed doing when I was talking with that new client?"

You'll return Suzie's call in a timely manner. You'll return the DVD to the store when it's due, avoiding late fees. You'll remember to get that order shipped out. You'll call David to tell him you can't make it to the concert Thursday night—on Tuesday. Nothing will slip your mind! Everything will be organized, saved, and secured in your emergency mental file the minute you think about it!

Give your memory some credit and it won't let you down. Wait, haven't I already said this? (Good, you're paying attention.)

BONUS: HOW TO REMEMBER TO DIET

There is a direct link between memory and dieting. Often attempts at losing weight fail because we simply forget that we're dieting. If a bowl of potato chips just happens to be in front of us, odds are we'll instinctively start to munch on them. Half an hour later, we'll realize our stomach is full. It's when we feel a little nauseous that we remember that—uh—we're on a diet.

Many times we eat simply because we feel it would be a shame not to. Mom made this great lasagna—pity to let it go to waste. Judy and Mark invited us over for a barbecue—how can we say no?

> Herb calls his mother in Florida.
>
> "How are you doing, Mom?" he inquires.
>
> "What can I say?" she sighs. "I haven't eaten anything for three months now."
>
> "Why not, Mama?"
>
> "Well, I just didn't want to have my mouth full when you finally called."

Of course we'll go. And then, twenty hamburgers and thirty hot dogs are left over—a crying shame. It's such a shame that we feel obligated to eat them. We get invited to a wedding and present the young couple with a generous check. We shouldn't waste the food they paid so much for. We must finish everything on our plate!

As we program our daily reminder system "software," we can add another command—one that will remind us to stay on the healthy eating track. This will help us avoid undesirable foods and, yes, succeed in losing weight.

First, it's important that we plan what we are going to eat for the day. We can't count on sitting down in a restaurant and then deciding what to order, because usually at a restaurant we're hungry and the instinct is to cut ourselves some slack. Just as we've done throughout this chapter, we'll use associations. We can start by associating the silverware with something else that will remind us that we are on a diet.

You could imagine that the last person to use the silverware was a repulsive, drooling man. Imagine the fork or spoon in his mouth, slobber hanging off the handle. This association should curb your appetite somewhat and remind you of your diet. In addition, you could create even more unpleasant associations. For most people, food is associatively linked to pleasure. This link must be changed. Associate unhealthy foods such as candy, pastries, and ice cream to feelings of pain or disgust. The purpose is to heighten our thoughts of guilt by using conditioning and associative links.

Imagine that ice cream is the number one cause of horrendous stomach cramps. Envision that there are large, slimy worms in the cookie jar. Imagine with each bite of the mega-size candy bar, your teeth will disintegrate a little more. As you remove that lollipop wrapper, imagine the thrill your dentist will have drilling inside your teeth with no anesthesia. When you browse the menu at a restaurant, envision the dessert section titled "Regretful High-Calorie Endings." While you consider the twelve-layer chocolate cake, imagine how painful and costly liposuction would be.

If this doesn't do the trick, you may need to resort to British comedian Benny Hill's diet advice: "You may eat everything you feel like eating, and at any time, as long as you don't swallow."

With time, the mental filing system will become purely habit. You'll find that you can go over the files in your mind as easily and instinctively as opening your calendar or turning on your BlackBerry. It's a whole new way of remembering what you have to do, and you can opt for any filing system of your choice.

You will also find that any new memory that pops in your head at the most inconvenient time can be dealt with later. You'll be able to link it quickly and efficiently to one of the items in your "sudden must-remember attack" room and be sure you'll find it there later.

With time you'll discover that you'll automatically begin filing away an assortment of thoughts, ideas, scenarios, and tasks for later use. And you'll no longer fear that your memory will not be able to handle it.

Excuse me now while I go and defrost some DVDs from the freezer. . . .

COMBATING FORGETFULNESS: THE KEY TO REMEMBERING THE KEYS

I THINK, THEREFORE I AM . . . I THINK.
—*Descartes, after four shots of bourbon*

WE ALL FALL prey to forgetfulness traps, such as talking on the phone while unpacking groceries and preparing dinner as the television news blares in the background. When we don't pay attention to what we're doing while we do it, we set ourselves up for not remembering a darn thing when we need to remember it.

Say we came home yesterday and plopped our keys down somewhere and, uh, we ended up forgetting what we did with those &#!%! keys.

But did we forget? Actually, no. We never remembered to begin with. As noted in Chapter 4, we simply weren't paying attention. Absentmindedly, we put down our keys while thinking of something else. We put the keys on a table, the sofa, or in some other random place. When we did this, there was a moment of disconnection between our memory and our hand's action of putting down the keys.

This problem doesn't only apply to keys. It involves other small items such as a pen we were holding, a comb, or eyeglasses.

Pay attention to an action while you're doing it and create an awareness of the situation. The minute you put down your glasses on the television, all you have to do is devote one second of awareness to this action: "I put the glasses down here." After establishing this awareness, create an associative conditioning between the action and your memory.

If you set down your Mont Blanc pen on the sofa's armrest, imagine that the pen is leaking red ink, staining your sofa. If you put down your glasses on the television, imagine they have explosive tendencies. Visualize your television set being blown to smithereens as soon as you lay your glasses on it. It's hard to forget about those glasses after that kind of mental imagery.

The best way, however, to remember where you put your belongings is simply by putting them where they belong.

When I was around fourteen years old, I had a brilliant idea one hot summer day. I decided to put my sandals in the freezer, behind packages of frozen meat, for several hours in order to enjoy cool soles as it sweltered outside.

The problem was that I totally forgot about them.

For several days I kept searching for my sandals, puzzled. Finally, one evening before dinner, a loud shout from the kitchen echoed throughout the house.

"Why in the name of God are there sandals in the freezer?"

I learned my lesson the hard way: always put your belongings in their proper, designated place.

Memory is a matter of habit. If years ago you baked a delicious cake using a recipe from a cookbook and haven't baked it since, you probably won't remember how to bake it today. But if you bake the same cake every few weeks, it's highly likely that you'll be able to bake it without a recipe, out of sheer habit.

Remember the habit we worked on at the beginning of the book, in chapter 4—locking the door and jiggling the handle to help remind ourselves that we did indeed lock the door? Here's another one: get used to putting your keys, glasses, or cell phone in a designated place, say, in a small porcelain bowl, a basket, or on a key hook next to the door.

You may also want to create an associative link between the keys and the bowl. For example, imagine that you have to recharge your keys, and that can be done only in the bowl. The minute you put your keys in the bowl, it sets off a mystical violet glow, which is cast onto the keys, energizing them. (Do you think I've seen *Superman* too many times?)

NEVER LOSE YOUR WALLET AGAIN

"Imagine your wallet as being sensitive to light," advised a banker in one of my seminars. "Your wallet must not be exposed to light for more than a few minutes."

"Why?" I asked curiously.

"Did you ever think about the fact that your wallet is kept in dark places most of the time? Your wallet is usually in your pocketbook, back pocket, or a drawer."

A wallet is kept in these places for a reason. This is so greedy people, unable to resist the temptation set before them, won't be able to "adopt" it as their own. The link between the wallet and light will remind you that you must put your wallet down in a safe haven. Imagine that the minute you take your wallet out of your purse, the countdown begins. Within seconds, your wallet will start to heat up and shrivel. Feel the heat on your fingers, which gets stronger until you put it back in its rightful place. This imagined sensation will prevent you from forgetting it on a restaurant table after paying the bill, for example.

When at home you could stow your wallet in the desk drawer and create an association between your wallet and the hollow sound it makes when you plop it down inside the wooden drawer. Once you establish this association, it will be impossible for your wallet *not* to generate this sound when it hits the bottom of the drawer.

Here's a scenario using this example: When you walk through the door and want to set your wallet down in a random place, you will be "attacked" by two sensations. One, your wallet will feel like it's burning in your hand. Two, you won't hear the plopping sound the wallet makes when dropped in the drawer. Combined,

A thief who broke into the house of the nineteenth-century French writer Honoré de Balzac. Once in the bedroom, the thief quietly searched the desk drawer for money until he heard someone giggle. Turning around, he spotted Balzac sitting in his bed, watching his every move and chuckling.

"What's so funny?" the surprised thief asked.

The famous writer answered: "It's funny you should think that you'll be able to find money inside the drawer in the middle of the night . . . something its legal owner isn't able to do during the day!"

these two sensations will remind you to put your wallet in its proper place.

These strategies sound great, but I assume you may be wondering: What can be done when we didn't remember to create an associative link as required, or the object is already missing?

REMEMBERING WHAT WE FORGOT

Where Did I Put Those Keys?

First, do *not* think about the object itself. Instead, think about the circumstances that led you to put it down somewhere. More specifically, you should think about what you intended to do.

Many times we try to think about what we did before we lost the object: "I walked through the door, went into the living room, and then the bathroom." But there's a more effective way to remember. Take one step back and try to remember what you *wanted* to do several minutes before you lost the object.

In the case of the disappearing keys, think of your plans prior to entering the house. For instance, what did you intend to do immediately upon stepping through the door? Maybe you were in a hurry to catch the beginning of your favorite television show. If so, perhaps you absentmindedly put your keys on the TV. Or as you were climbing up the stairs to your apartment, you thought about a book that your friend asked to borrow, so you concentrated on how you needed to put it in your bag as soon as you walked in the door so that you wouldn't forget it. Could it be that you put your keys on the bookshelf? Go one step back, but don't recall what you were doing—recall what you *wanted* to do.

Where Did We Park the Car?

This may be obvious, but when parking your car, you've got to pay attention to the place where you parked. Search for reference points nearby which will remind you of its location. This may be a large tree, a billboard, or the number and color of the level you parked on.

You can turn that action into an associative habit. Imagine that every time you get out of the car, shut the door, and lock it, you need to do a 360-degree spin. Imagine this as an exaggerated ballet-type rotational movement. Such a ridiculous thought will remind you that the purpose of the spin is to examine your new location and pay attention to your surroundings.

If you didn't pay attention, try to remember what you were thinking about while you were driving. Perhaps you wanted to park close to a specific place but were disappointed to find all the spaces there full. So maybe you went up to the second level and were disappointed again when another car pulled into the one vacant spot just before you could. If so, that may be how you ended up parking on the third level.

But where did *Noah* park his "car'? We'll get to that later, don't worry . . .

USING REMINDERS

Did you ever notice the following sign in a restaurant restroom?

EMPLOYEES MUST WASH HANDS BEFORE
RETURNING TO WORK.

An obvious fact, isn't it? I think we should have similar signs for other professions:

BUS DRIVERS MUST HOLD ON TO STEERING
WHEEL WHILE DRIVING.

SALESPEOPLE MUST BRUSH TEETH BEFORE
TALKING TO CUSTOMERS.

UNDERTAKERS MUST APPEAR DEPRESSED
BEFORE ATTENDING A FUNERAL.

I always thought the bathroom sign was a publicity stunt. You know, as if it was declaring, "No need to fear—we are a clean and hygienic dining facility because all of us constantly wash our hands around here." Perhaps the sign does have a certain PR effectiveness, but its main purpose, as surprising as it sounds, is actually to remind employees to wash their hands! With all their good intentions, kitchen workers are human beings like the rest of us, who may ponder their latest love affair while rushing back to work after relieving themselves . . . and forgetting to wash their hands.

Sometimes we all need a reminder of our everyday tasks. For example, we all want to remember to be at our child's school exactly at the time they need to be picked up. If we know we'll be preoccupied with something, we should use a reminder to make sure we make it to the school at the correct time. An easy solution is to set a timer that will go off when we need to leave to pick up Luigi (our progeny).

If you turn on the washing machine and want to remember to transfer the wet clothes to the dryer before you leave the house, tie a plastic bag filled with some detergent on the doorknob. When you start to head out, your visual reminder will send you to the laundry room first.

If you need to remember to take medicine twice a day, link

it to another task you do twice a day—brushing your teeth, for example.

In case you're now done reading for the day, please place this book in its *proper* place once you close it—say, on the nightstand next to your bed, or on a shelf. Do not—I repeat, do not—put it in the freezer.

~~~~~~~~~~~~~~~~

CHAPTER 11

HOW TO REMEMBER ANY NUMBER, ANYTIME

TAKE NOTE OF the following number:

4803756293075650202188509384573892020
3484565634389230208405575849493020102
9283746564748430374936582029845638 39
2047984638002765689320485654830012846

You will soon be able to remember this number or any other random collection of dozens or hundreds of digits. And you'll achieve this by going over such a number only once.

I'll reiterate. A number, made up of a hundred digits, will be read to you once. Afterward, you will be able to repeat it from beginning to end, and from the end to the beginning.

At this moment, you might feel like Groucho Marx, who once said: *"From the moment I picked your book up until I laid it down, I was convulsed with laughter. Someday I intend reading it.*" But I stand behind every word you have just read. I always demonstrate this stunt in my lectures and seminars. Usually the audience is stunned. People come up to me and say things like "What an amazing memory!" "When did you discover you have a phenomenal memory?" "Would you like to date my daughter?" "Would you consider replacing my husband?"

Throughout the ego massage, I'm smiling inside. I'm thinking about my wife, who makes fun of my "phenomenal memory" every time I fail to remember that we're scheduled to go out with some friends. (Actually, I do remember, but I'm hopeful she'll forget and we won't need to go out.)

People are amazed by such a trick because it seems an impossible task for the human memory. We're impressed by the extraordinary; we cannot grasp things that seem to be illogical.

David Copperfield, the famous magician, is able to make a train car disappear into thin air, an impossible act. But when we see the train car disappear in front of our very eyes, it is possible. All we are dealing with is a magic trick, and a magic trick is purely an optical illusion.

If someone explained to you how every magic trick was actually performed, you'd probably say: "Ah, that's no big deal." It's the same with "memory magic." I will teach you how to perform this magic and easily remember a hundred-digit number as well as any number-related data such as phone numbers, credit card numbers, PINs, ID numbers, historical dates, and financial figures.

You may not believe me, but remembering a hundred-digit number isn't such a complicated memory stunt. It's really quite simple. Each and every one of us is capable of doing this, including your daughter *and* your husband.

THE ART OF CONVERTING NUMBERS INTO WORDS

So what is the trick to remembering numbers?

Not remembering them.

Well, what I mean is you replace the numbers with letters. Let's begin with a brief history of the number-letter method.

Numbers, on their own, are difficult to remember or to imagine in an interesting way. That's why most of us find number recall an especially complicated task. Usually the only time we remember a number is when it holds a special meaning or has something to do with us. Since most of us have a hard time remembering numbers that mean nothing to us, scholars throughout the ages have searched for a "memorable" solution to the problem.

One excellent solution was to assign letters to numbers and thus create words, because the good thing about words is that they make sense.

The ancient Greeks, Romans, and Egyptians assigned visual graphic value to numbers, but this was not good enough to create words. The Jews came up with *gematria* (probably derived from the Greek word *geometria*). The idea is to basically assign the first letter of the Hebrew alphabet, aleph, to the first number, 1; the second letter, bet, to the second number, 2; and so on.

Gematria is popular even today in religious Jewish circles, where it is usually implemented to find mystical meanings in different numeral combinations. The best-known example of Jewish *gematria* is the number 18, which symbolizes the word "life" (*chai*, חי). The number 18 is a combination of the numbers 8 (ח) + 10 (י) = "life." This number is considered lucky, and it's common practice to give checks for certain celebrations (weddings, bar mitzvahs) in multiples of 18 ($180, or 360 Israeli shekels, or 18 trillion Japanese yen).

Gematria was not necessarily intended to assist the memory, but the first person who actually did think of using the number-letter method for memory purposes was Stanislaus Mink von Wennsshein (also known as J. J. Winkelmann) in 1648. Von Wennsshein assigned each digit from 0 to 9 a common letter from the alphabet as a sort of code to help remember numbers. The code was later revised by Gregor von Feinaigle, a German monk, in 1811. However, the first to prove the efficiency of this code as a memory system was Major Beniowski in 1832, a Pole who lived in London and earned fame by demonstrating outstanding memory stunts. Beniowski attracted thousands who came to see his phenomenal ability to remember endless series of random numbers. Memory artists today continue using this method, and so can you. You are cordially invited to join the family!

Here's the code as Beniowski wrote it in his *Handbook of Phrenotypics for Teachers and Students*. Please pay close attention to it. I will explain afterward how it works and demonstrate its fantastic uses.

0	S, Z, soft C (as in *ceremony*)	Remember as "Z is first letter of *zero*"
1	D, T, TH	Remember the letters D and T have 1 downstroke
2	N	Remember the letter has 2 downstrokes

3	M	Remember the letter has three downstrokes
4	R	Imagine a 4 and an R glued together back to back
5	L	Roman letter for 50 (L)
6	J, SH, soft CH (as in *chandelier*), soft G (as in *gene*)	G looks very similar to the number 6
7	K, hard CH (as in *charisma*), hard C (as in *cat*), hard G (as in *gray*)	Imagine K as two 7's rotated and glued together
8	F, V	Imagine the bottom loop of the 8 as an effluent pipe discharging waste (letter image of F in alphabet system)
9	P, B	P as a mirror reflection of 9

We'll use vowels (A, E, I, O, U) to give the consonants meaning. If it's necessary to use other consonants to make up a word, use only those that aren't already coded with numbers, such as H, Q, X, and Y.

Let's take 21, for example. We will create a word in the order in which we read the digits, from left to right. So 21 is NT (2 = N, 1 = T). Now let's add a letter (from A, E, I, O, U, H, Q, X, or Y) in order to come up with an actual word: *nut* or *note*.

Flip 21 around and you've got 12, which is made up of the letters T and N; add a letter from our list and you've got *tan*, *tone*, or *tune*.

Here are some more examples:

> 22 (2 = N, 2 = N) = *nun*
> 49 (4 = R, 9 = P, B) = *rope*
> 216 (2 = N, 1 = D, T, TH, 6 = J, SH, soft CH, soft G) =
> *nudge*

When we want to translate a word back to numbers, we give each coded consonant its number. For instance, what number will we get if we break down the word *beer*? Remember, vowels are only connectors. We must convert the letters B and R to numbers: B = 9, R = 4. We get 94.

What is *castle*? C = 7, S = 0, T = 1, L = 5: *castle* is 7015.

What is 8197? Can you figure it out yourself? I'll give you a hint: it's the opposite of a 'thin book'. Please check.

Now, let's practice this method and file it in our long-term memory.

Exercise 1: Turning Digits into Words

Turn the following digits into words that can be easily imagined. Make use of A, E, I, O, and U in order to make up the words.

Here are a few examples:

76	*cash*	Imagine a wallet stuffed with cash
97	*bug*	Imagine an annoying bug buzzing around your ear
58	*love*	Imagine someone you love
85	*file*	Imagine a manila file containing important information

74	*car*	Imagine a red sports car
13	*dime*	Imagine holding a dime in your hand
65	*jail*	Imagine being in jail
30	*maze*	Imagine a mirror maze in the amusement park
974	*poker*	Imagine four men sitting around a table in a smoky room, playing poker
41	*red*	Imagine a red flag
687	*jfk*	Imagine John F. Kennedy with Marilyn Monroe, or the crowded New York City airport

If two or more words pop into your mind, write them down. Remember that the words must be real. For example, 91 is BD, BT, PT, or PD. Don't think about what the letter pairs might mean. Try to add A, E, I, O, U in the beginning, middle, or at the end of the word, and then you can turn BD into *bed*, or BT into *bat*, *bet*, or *bad*.

One more thing: try to choose words that are concrete rather than abstract. The number 91 can be *bed*, *bat*, or *bad*. *Bad* is an example of an abstract word that is difficult to imagine vividly. *Bed*, on the other hand, is easier to picture—just think of your own bed. Or imagine a bat flying above your bed at night, a breeze from its wings sweeping across your face. So it is much preferred to turn 91 into *bed* versus *bad*.

Keep going with this. Feel free to write inside the book itself—that's what it's meant for. (And it's also great for me, the publisher, and the entire book industry, because once you write in it, you can't return it to the bookstore . . . but you wouldn't do that anyhow, right? I mean, we have established good rapport during the last eleven chapters, haven't we?)

Have fun with the following exercises:

31 _____
32 _____
48 _____
67 _____
59 _____
95 _____
07 _____
990 _____
33 _____
37 _____
51 _____
88 _____
12 _____
90 _____

Exercise 2: Turning Words into Digits

Take out the letters A, E, I, O, U, W, H, Q, X, Y when they appear in the words on the next page. Change the rest of the letters in the words into digits. For example (see next page):

rubber	4994	*mug*	37
lettuce	5110	*sculpture*	075914
canopy	729	*bagel*	975
hail	5	*mail*	35
dollar	1554		

Now continue on your own:

John _____

Clinton (as in Bill Clinton)_____

lottery _____

Snoopy _____

Seinfeld _____

*copper*_____

magnolia _____

*poodle*_____

bee _____

scarecrow _____

map _____

*rope*_____

pub _____

oyster _____

garlic _____

bench _____

cavalier _____

playpen _____

A reminder of the key:

0 = S, Z, soft C	**5** = L
1 = D, T,TH	**6** = J, SH, soft CH, soft G
2 = N	**7** = K, hard CH, hard C, hard G
3 = M	**8** = F, V
4 = R	**9** = P, B

WHERE DID NOAH PARK THE ARK?

flag _____

drug_____

liver _____

hollow _____

confusion_____

doll _____

gold _____

Buddha _____

Exercise 3: Combining the Previous Two Exercises

Turn the following words into digits, and the following numbers into words. For example:

academy 713   fruit 841
3742 migraine   43 room

Now, continue on your own:

17 _____

22_____

19 _____

popcorn_____

bear _____

234 _____

horse _____

car wash _____

36 _____

80 _____

screwdriver _____

09 _____

5,681 _____

jelly _____

547 _____

spirit _____

OO _____

*generation*_____

247_____

*allergy*_____

This method is not culturally binding. It simply means that you may add to a certain word any letter you wish, or any other changes you feel are helpful. If a certain combination of letters works better for you in another language, don't try to find its meaning in English. For example, 955 may be *bell* in English (the kind that rings) or *ball* (the kind you kick). Someone else may find it easier to remember it as *bella* ("beauty" in Italian). Do whatever makes this method easier for you—just make sure that the change won't confuse you.

And now for the big question: How do we put this method to good use?

A reminder of the key:

0 = S, Z, soft C	**5** = L
1 = D, T,TH	**6** = J, SH, soft CH, soft G
2 = N	**7** = K, hard CH, hard C, hard G
3 = M	**8** = F, V
4 = R	**9** = P, B

CHAPTER 12

KING SOLOMON'S PHONE BOOK

The parents of a sixteen-year-old girl despair over her long phone conversations with her many friends. Each phone call lasts an average of forty-five minutes.

One day they're surprised to hear their daughter end a conversation after twenty minutes.

"What's wrong? Twenty minutes, that's it?" the father sarcastically asks.

"It was a wrong number," the teenager answers.

KING SOLOMON HAD a thousand wives, probably four thousand daughters, five thousand sons, nine thousand cousins, and three masseuses. That's an awful lot of phone numbers to remember . . . and a huge phone bill! (Of course, he didn't pay. He was the king.)

It's fine to keep phone numbers in your phone book, Black-Berry, or cell phone. This is a first step. However, after you've recorded the numbers, transfer them into your long-term memory.

Yes, I'm talking about the one tucked away in the depths of your mind. Don't panic—you don't need to memorize all phone numbers, only the important ones. It's possible and it's important. (I'll explain why later.) To do this, we'll implement the number-letter method we just learned in the previous chapter, and see for ourselves that it's an amazing memory tool.

We already know how to turn digits into words and words into digits. The purpose of this method is to convert every phone number into a visual image and associate it with the number's owner.

> Operator: "411 directory assistance, how may I help you?"
>
> You: "Could you please give me the telephone number for Dr. James Green, dentist, 58 Wisteria Lane, in Creepville, Kentucky?"
>
> Operator: "Thank you, sir. Have a nice day."
>
> Recording: "The number is . . . 0-1-7 . . ."
>
> You: "Quick, where's the pen? Harry? C'mon!"
>
> Recording: "5-1-2 . . ."
>
> You: "Wait!"
>
> Recording: "3-2 . . ."
>
> You: "Oh no . . ."
>
> Recording: "9-9 . . ."
>
> You: "Harry! The pen! *Now!*"

Relax. There's no need to panic—you really don't need a pen. Pay close attention.

> Recording: "017 . . ."
>
> You: "Okay, that's Creepville, I know that." (Assuming you do.)

Recording: "5-1-2 . . ."
You: "5 = L; 1 = D, T, TH; 2 = N—*Latin*."
Recording: "3-2 . . ."
You: "3 = M; 2 = N—*man*."
Recording: ". . . 9-9 . . ."
You: "9 = P, B; 9 = P, B—*pub*."
Recording: "I repeat . . ."
You, happily: "That will not be necessary. I've got it."

"Latin man in a pub" can be the phrase created by converting Dr. Green's phone number using this system.

Now we have to create an associative bond between Dr. Green and the words *Latin*, *man*, and *pub*. For example, you could imagine Dr. Green, his hands working away in the mouth of a big Latino man in the middle of a pub, after giving him a lot of beer as an anesthetic. (It was an emergency call, and Dr. Green was the first dentist ever to perform a root canal surrounded by dozens of cheering, drunk *mochileros*.) This image is quite amusing, don't you think?

Suddenly the phone rings. Michelle is on the line. She heads into this never-ending monologue about her brother. He just returned from his business trip and failed to remember to buy her the iPod he had promised. Before we get a chance to say anything, she starts telling us about the movie she saw last week. It was Robert Redford's *The Horse Whisperer*. She spares us no detail of the movie, saving us from spending our money at the theater. At one point, we apologize for being in a hurry to call the dentist in order to schedule an appointment before his clinic closes for the day. The conversation finally ends and the phone remains in our hand—now on to Dr. Green.

Where did we write down his number? We try to remember and start to shuffle through the papers scattered on the desk.

Oh no, we didn't write the number down. But we do remember the call to directory assistance, and we realize that we tried to recall the number. Let's see if the method worked. We decide to give it a shot before calling directory assistance again.

What was the story with Dr. Green? He was giving a dental treatment to a Latino man in a pub. Ha!

"Latin man in a pub"—we become excited. Those were the words!

L becomes 5 (press 5)
T becomes 1 (press 1)
N becomes 2 (press 2)
M becomes 3 (press 3)
N becomes 2 (press 2)
P becomes 9 (press 9)
B becomes 9 (press 9)

After a few seconds, a voice answers on the other end: "Dr. Green's clinic, Debbie speaking . . ."

"Well, I'll be darned," you reply. "The method really works!"

You can divide phone numbers into two, three, or four words—whatever combination works better for you. Let's say we scribbled Jeff's phone number—508-372-1692—on a scrap of paper. First, there's no need to convert 508, or any other area code, into a word. We usually know where the person we are looking for lives or works, so the area code shouldn't be a problem to remember on its own. As for the rest of the digits: 37216 = *Macintosh* (!), 92 = *pin*. We could imagine Jeff talking on the phone while working on his Macintosh that is covered with pins.

You could split the number in a different way: 37 = *mug*;

21 = *note*; 692 = *Chopin*. In this case, imagine Jeff picking up the phone while holding a mug with a note stuck to it, as one of Chopin's symphonies plays in the background. While this is definitely a silly thought totally unrelated to Jeff and his musical tastes, it's exactly the reason it will help us remember his phone number, or anybody else's, for that matter.

OTHER WAYS TO REMEMBER PHONE NUMBERS

It's important to note that the number-letter method doesn't rule out other methods you may find helpful. If it's easy and convenient for you to remember the phone number 555-8765 and it makes mathematical sense (the last four digits are in descending order), don't force the digits into words.

There are some people who find it easy to remember phone numbers by each digit's placement on the phone and the order of pressing each button—meaning the geometrical order:

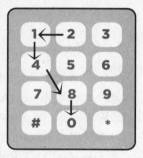

The number-letter method is meant to help when a phone number is complicated and difficult to remember, which is nearly always the case. How many phone numbers do you know that look like 688-8888? Not too many, I suppose. (You can combine a few methods too, if you'd like. Try using mathematical combinations or geometrical shapes.)

Take, for example, the phone number of the local library: 617-690-8888. We will use our method to convert the first part into a word: 690 can become *chops*. It isn't necessary to convert the second part into words—it's easy to remember.

Now we have to associate it to the library. So let's imagine that a famous chef is at the library to promote his new cookbook and is demonstrating fancy maneuvers with a sharp knife and vegetables of all kinds. What does he do? He chops.

Take a few minutes now to convert the ten phone numbers which are most important to you. When you're done, sear them into your long-term memory by creating an associative link to the owner of the phone number. Do not use phone numbers that are already ingrained in your memory, such as your home phone number, office phone number, or best friend's cell phone number; choose numbers that you don't use so often.

Name	Phone Number	Words	Image (description of the associative link)
Airport taxi	79-79-800-77	*cab-cap-fuss-cake*	A cab driver wearing a cap is making a fuss over a cake left in the cab

Go over the list again, and make sure that you firmly established the words and associations in your mind.

WHY BOTHER?

"Why should I make the effort to do this," you may be asking, "when our cell phones have all of the phone numbers we need, stored neatly away in their memory cards?"

There are several answers:

1. A cell phone will not become demented due to lack of brain usage when it gets old.
2. A cell phone can get lost. A mind won't.
3. I will take it very personally if you don't try out these methods.

But seriously, it will save you precious time when you recall numbers from your own memory, and it will generate a sense of self-confidence, self-control, and self-satisfaction. Plus, it will make a really good impression on other people. Most important, you'll have fun memorizing numbers!

My advice to you is as follows:

1. For starters, program just one new phone number every day in your mind. After you do so, go over the numbers you have already "stored." View this as an amusing way to kill time while you're on the bus, in the car, or sitting in Dr. Green's waiting room as you imagine yourself tossing back a few beers before you get your teeth examined by the infamous pub dentist. (This also can be a good method to help distract you from any fears you may have of going to the dentist.)

2. Close your eyes and think: "What have I done with X's phone number?" Go over it in your mind and visually see

the connection between the number and the person. If you are unable to recall the number, this means the link—the image in your mind—isn't strong enough. All you have to do is strengthen that link.

3. Practice one new number every day, as well as two old ones. At first this will take you perhaps five minutes. Later on, as you develop this skill, the time it will take you will be much shorter.

4. After you've imprinted all the numbers in your memory, continue the recall exercise once every two weeks—there's no need to do so more often than that.

You will be delighted to find that with some practice, you can remember all the phone numbers that are important to you. You will be able to retrieve them from your memory anytime you wish. This will hold true even if a few months pass since you last dialed the number.

~~~~~~~~~~~~~~~~

CHAPTER 13

FROM THE LOUISIANA PURCHASE TO NAPOLEON'S SHOE SIZE

HISTORY IS THE
SUM TOTAL OF ALL THINGS THAT
COULD HAVE BEEN AVOIDED.
—*Konrad Adenauer*

I DON'T KNOW if Konrad Adenauer, the first chancellor of the Federal Republic of Germany, was right. But in any case, it doesn't really matter. The past cannot be changed. We can, however, change our attitude when it comes to remembering historic events.

We'll learn how to easily remember historical facts in Chapter 15. In this chapter, we'll concentrate on remembering historical dates, birthdays, measurements, and other important numerical information.

Someone who remembers the exact date of an event being discussed surely deserves admiration. This is simply because it's difficult to remember numbers in general and specific dates in particular. Not long ago I met with the manager of an SAT preparation school. We were talking about memory improvement when he suddenly asked me: "Tell me, do you happen to remember what you were doing on October 3, 1995?"

"I have no idea, and there is no reason for me to remember what I did on that date or another date so many years ago," I replied.

"Exactly," he said. "But do you remember what you were doing on September 11, 2001?"

We all probably remember very well where we were and what we were doing when we heard the horrifying news of terrorist attacks in New York and Washington, DC. As soon as a connection is made, a date is given meaning and we remember it. In order to remember historical events, we need to find meaning in the date on which the event took place.

Just as it is with certain phone numbers, it may be that certain dates are associated with numbers that have specific meaning for you. The year of the French Revolution—1789—may be easily remembered as it contains the sequence 7, 8, 9. It could be even easier for you to remember if your history class in high school was held in room 17.

If the date has no meaning, we can make use of the number-letter method we just learned. All we have to do is convert the dates into one or more words. So let's split the date in two: 17, 89. Then 17 becomes *dog* and 89 becomes *VIP*. Now imagine that on the date of the French Revolution, as the Bastille gates became battered and broken, all the dogs who'd kept watch of them took out their guest lists. As they checked them, they let the VIP French prisoners out with no further questions. Yes, it was simple to get past the dogs if you were a VIP. And that's how the French Revolution took place.

Say you wish to know the exact date of the Boston Tea Party. Imagine the crates of tea drifting toward the Massachusetts shore, followed by one **ton** of tea-leaf-constructed **shoes** to the excitement of Native American **dogs**; until that point, the poor mutts had to make do with chewing **gum**. When we convert *ton*, *tea*, *shoe*, *dog*, and *gum* into digits we have T, N, T, SH, D, G, G, M, which brings us to 12-16-1773, the date on which the Boston Tea Party took place!

World War I broke out in 1914. We know that the event occurred in the twentieth century, so there is no need to remember 19 in an extraordinary way. All we have to do is convert 14 to a word—*door*. Now imagine a huge door swinging open and for the first time in the world's history, warplanes fly out in mass numbers, along with cannonballs and smoke. Once you have this vivid image of the war door down pat, convert it back into 14 and you've got the date you wanted to remember—1914.

I don't know Napoleon's shoe size, but it's easy to remember the years in which he ruled as emperor. Imagine Napoleon wearing his much-needed visor when he was crowned and finishing his career in a fatal way. *Visor* = 804, *fatal* = 815. It was in the last millennium, so we will add the 1, and discover that Napoleon was emperor between the years 1804 and 1815.

If you wish to remember the year in which the world's first astronomer, Nicolaus Copernicus, died, imagine that when his passing was discovered, an ear-piercing alarm was sounded all over the land. *Alarm* = 543. Because it's in the first millennium, you add a 1. So now you know that Nicolaus Copernicus died in 1543.

MEASUREMENTS

Those of you who are studying geography should find this method helpful for remembering heights, areas, and distances.

How long is the Amazon River? Imagine that this great body of water is highly polluted with junk and other goo. *Junk*, *goo* (J, N, K, G) = 6,277 kilometers. By the way, for your general knowledge, this river is so great that at its outfall into the ocean, its width is 600 kilometers, almost a tenth of its length!

Now imagine you are strolling along the Champs-Elysees in Paris and casually enter a fancy shoe boutique. "Wow, this is great!" you think. "Sheila asked me to buy her a pair of red Pradas. This is a wonderful chance to get that purchase out of the way."

You approach the saleswoman, who has a fine French scowl plastered across her face, and ask her: *"Avez-vous des chaussures Prada, en rouge?"* Do you have red Prada shoes?

She frowns and leads you to the correct shelf. *"Quelle taille?"* What size?

"Oh, no!" you mutter to yourself. "What's Sheila's shoe size?"

You wrote it down in your notebook . . . which is at the hotel. How annoying! You'll just have to come back another time.

But there's really no need to go back and waste your time. As soon as Sheila tells you that her European shoe size is 39, convert it to the word *mob*. Imagine Sheila sending out the Mob to get you if you buy her the wrong shoe size . . . some kind of friend she is!

Now, as you stand before the lovely saleslady, there's no need to feel frustrated because you left your notebook at the hotel. Just think about the Mob chasing you if you dare bring the wrong shoes (*mob* = 39).

"*Trente-neuf,*" you proudly exclaim, contorting your mouth muscles to properly pronounce every syllable.

The saleslady brings out a luxuriously designed shoe box and places it on the counter. "That will be seven thousand euros," she says calmly.

"*Ah, oui,*" you murmur. "Actually . . . I need to check on the size again with my friend." You're sweating now. "I'll come back tomorrow . . . or next week. Probably next week . . . or in my next life," you add over your shoulder as you bolt out the door and into the street.

WHAT PAGE WAS I ON?

On page 83—give or take a hundred pages . . .

As has been mentioned incessantly, the most efficient way to remember something is to pay attention. Thus, the best way to remember what page we were on is to take a look at it as we put the book down.

In most cases, we set down a book without paying much attention. But one minute of attention to the fact that we're on page 83 will remind us later to open the book to that page. Or you could convert the page number, 83, into *foam*. Imagine you have to wipe the foam from your bubble bath off the book cover. (Yes, this might ruin the book a bit, but it will surely help you to remember.)

I realize the number-letter method seems a bit complicated, and I am willing to take a wild guess that most of you won't be using it. That's too bad, because it's actually a really fun method. Sometimes you can come up with mystical meanings to certain numbers. For example, when a friend of mine got married, his new home phone number turned out to be, when converted to letters, something like T R B L M R R G—which is (gulp) *terrible marriage*. I never told him about this and he actually has a happy and successful marriage, but every time I call him and his wife, I can't stop smiling.

Go ahead and have fun. Convert a few numbers just for laughs. Who knows, maybe you'll also discover a whole new world of mystical codes tucked innocently away among your numbers.

Here, try to remember these important dates as an exercise:

528 B.C.	Siddhartha Gautama (Buddha) is enlightened
October 1, 1949	Chairman Mao proclaims the People's Republic of China
1295	Marco Polo's second voyage to the Far East
1492	Columbus sails to America

And remember these?

1776	The American Revolution
1815	The Battle of Waterloo
1974	Sammy Davis Jr.'s bar mitzvah
1917	The Russian Revolution
1770	Beethoven's birth
1932	Donald Duck's birth

CHAPTER 14

A SUPER MEMORY FOR STUDIES AND EXAMS

Eight Rules for Success in School

WHEN THE STUDENT IS READY, THE MASTER APPEARS.
—*Buddhist proverb*

WHEN I WAS in high school, the complete opposite of this proverb was true. It was only when I finally did do my homework that the teacher was out sick. Naturally, when I came to class unprepared, the teacher showed up—Eran Katz's Murphy's law.

Seriously, though, the above saying is one of the most beautiful and correct thoughts I know. Only if we truly want to learn is it possible for us to do so. If we don't—if we're not interested in the subject at hand, or if our learning environment (social or physical) is an unpleasant one—even the best of teachers won't do us any good.

Human instinct is to learn, and the intellectual stimulation of understanding and knowing is a payoff in and of itself. Yet often studying is associated with the terms *duty* (compulsory education), *existential necessity* (acquiring a profession), *pressure*, *competition*, *pain*, and *emotional distress*. All these terms express our state of mind, mainly because the quantity of learning material that has to be mastered is often inhuman. We recoil when the pressure of exams becomes unbearable. We feel exasperated when it seems to us that everyone else is a better student than we are. It seems to us that everyone else has better study habits, and for sure knows something that continues to elude us—and that something will surely be on the exam. Sound familiar?

Enough is enough. No more suffering! Allow me to tell you how to turn your study experience from pain into pleasure. Let me show you how to make it possible to study efficiently and without pressure. I will teach you how to remember tremendous amounts of material in half the time you are used to right now.

But first of all, a warning: this chapter may shock some readers. It promotes somewhat unusual ideas that might seem immoral to the conservatives among you.

On the other hand, students of higher education will probably rejoice in this chapter. It will legitimize what you've probably always dreamed of doing.

If you are concerned that this chapter might rock the foundations upon which you were raised, you're welcome to skip over to the next chapter. You can opt instead to continue to study in the conventionally boring way—to sit for long hours and learn information by heart.

THE YOUNG AND THE RESTLESS:
A PERSONAL STORY ABOUT LEARNING

Who feels like doing homework and sitting in class when the alternatives are to play ball, go to parties, have fun, and spend time with the boy- or girlfriend?

I didn't.

This is how I found myself spending long hours outside the walls of my high school. My grades were reflective of my behavior; I constantly received low marks. The ones I remember specifically: F in math, F in English, Z in history, and so on. The highest grade I ever got was an A in philosophy. The teacher said I deserved an A in this class because I successfully managed to prove to her that I didn't exist.

During the ninth grade, I was absent an average of three days a week. Twice a week I spent the early morning hours at the beach in Haifa, Israel, where I grew up. I read an article in which experts emphasized the importance of sunbathing when the sun's rays weren't harmful, sometime between 7:00 and 11:00 a.m. At 11:30, when the sun's rays became harmful, there was no point in going to school anymore, since I'd already missed most of the day.

One day the principal called me to his office.

"Young Mr. Katz, will it really kill you if you come to school on time?"

"I don't know, sir," I replied, after giving it some serious thought. "But it's a risk I'm not willing to take."

For this reason and others, my parents were summoned to school on occasion. Every parent-teacher conference day, my parents were notified diplomatically of the same diagnosis: "He has great potential, but it's wasted. He could achieve high grades if he wanted." And so my parents decided to grant me an incentive package: if I showed up at school every day, got normal grades, and did well on my SATs, I would get a monthly ticket to the movies, three season tickets for my basketball team, driving lessons at the end of the year, and a subscription to *Penthouse* magazine (my dad's idea, really— he said it had great feature articles that would improve my English). All this as long as I showed up at school every day and got decent grades.

When I was a junior in high school, a miracle happened. My mom bought me a book on how to perform memory stunts, written by Harry Lorayne. I read the book and became enthusiastic about it. I started performing memory stunts for a bunch of friends, just to show off.

One day it occurred to me that these exercises might actually be helpful for studying. Perhaps it would be possible to implement these techniques instead of exerting myself? To my great joy, it was possible. Thanks to these methods I graduated from high school without much effort.

Later on, I enrolled in university. When I arrived on campus it didn't even cross my mind to change my hedonistic habits. While my goal was to get a B.A., there was no reason I couldn't do so while having a good time.

I quickly found out that what was good for high school was even better for college. While my friends pulled all-nighters studying for exams, I learned the same material in a day or two. While my friends were under great pressure and stress, I felt guilty for not freaking out. I even waited for the exams! I felt eager to release the material I'd learned onto paper, and prove the capabilities of my trained memory.

In some of the exams, I even had the strange sensation that

I was somehow cheating, because it felt as though the material stored in my memory was equivalent to an open book in front of me.

At this point, I must note that I do not have a phenomenal memory and that I am of average intelligence. (My mother believes it's above average and my wife thinks it's below . . . which makes it exactly average.) The only asset at my disposal—which most of the other students I knew didn't have—was a trained memory. My memory was trained with the techniques you've learned by now, and will continue to learn as we progress in this book.

There are two types of students: the typical student who fights against time and pressure, and the student who enjoys his college years, studies in minimal time, and learns efficiently and with a sane amount of effort. As I stated before, you will be able to do all that if you wish—and if you have no fear!

Let's begin by getting acquainted with several rules for efficient studying. In order to present these, we will have to break several unnecessary and incorrect social and educational expectations.

THE EIGHT RULES FOR BECOMING
A SUCCESS IN SCHOOL

Rule #1: There Are No Rules

Is the majority correct?

The "rule of the herd" states that if everybody takes a certain path, it's probably the right path to take. If, in the middle of the desert among the endless vast dunes, you see a path created by dozens of footprints, it's probable that you will chose to follow it.

The first person who crossed this dune had no idea where his path would lead. He may have chosen the longest route, and if he had walked in a different direction he would have arrived at his destination much faster. The next person to arrive at the same starting point will see the footprint path and think: "Maybe this person knew where he was going, and anyway, I will surely see him at the end of the path." And so the second person follows the first person's path. The next people to arrive follow the same pattern. As more take this path, the deeper the footprints will become, and the more we will be convinced that this is in fact the correct path. It is only at the end of the path that we'll find the dried-up remains of all those who came before us and were stranded on a dead-end path in the middle of the desert.

If most Europeans in the Middle Ages thought that the earth was flat, then surely it was flat.

If most of our friends study quietly in their rooms or in the library, should it be clear that this is the correct way to study?

If our friends begin studying five days before an exam, then we naturally conclude that this is the requisite amount of time to prepare, and if we do not follow their lead, then we'll fall behind and have good reason to panic.

If everyone sits in class and vigorously writes down everything the lecturer says, then this must be the best way to summarize the lecture.

My answer to all of these examples is *not true*.

Everybody was convinced that the earth was flat—except for Copernicus.

A quiet study environment isn't necessarily the best environment in which to study.

There's no need to study five days for an exam simply because that's what everybody else is doing."

And the custom of writing down everything the lecturer says in class is a mistake that millions of students all over the world make every day.

Così fan tutte—"thus do they all"—is the most castrating phrase in the world.

Our study habits are based upon the way we were taught and upon what we see around us. At a very young age, we learned that it's good to make use of the early morning hours for studying. We were told that silence helps concentration. It was stressed that it's important to attend all classes. But the truth is much more complex and individualistic. Each one of us is different; we each have our own unique character traits, areas of interest, capabilities, and tempos.

Many high schools allow students to choose their course of study. He who loves animals may take more biology classes. She who takes a liking to reading can register for more creative writing or history courses. Those who take pride in disassembling the home entertainment system will find their place in mechanics.

However, in most schools, the student doesn't have the option of choosing the pace of study that best suits him. Most schools do not offer students the possibility of selecting the study method that fits them best as individuals.

We enter a learning program with so much enthusiasm, yet slowly we begin to hand-cuff ourselves. We become prisoners—prisoners of our own pressure.

We become stressed mainly through our social environment and the impending exam schedule. Beginning on the first day of class, we enter into this mode of imagined competition because our study peers stress us out just by the sake of existing.

Rule #2: There Is No Competition

We are always comparing ourselves to other students who seem smart and intimidating. Their notebooks are thicker than ours, their expressions more serious. If we miss a lecture, we're sure it must have been the most important lecture of the semester. We feel nervous when everybody takes thorough notes throughout the lecturer's speech and we aren't up to speed. And we lose our minds completely when finals arrive. Everyone around us is studying and persevering with incredible efficiency, maximizing their time.

When we ask a friend if he understood Kaufman's article, he sadistically answers: "Ah, that was easy. However, I did have some trouble with Johansson's book."

"What?" We are shell-shocked. "Johansson? We were supposed to read Johansson's book? Oh no, I didn't read Johansson's book. We were really supposed to read Johansson's entire book?"

Sound familiar?

Get some perspective. Don't get worked up over the students around you and the methods by which they study.

They are not better than you.

They are not more successful than you.

The so-called correct method by which they study isn't relevant to you at all! High school and college are not an *American Idol* competition with one final winner. "And the A goes to . . ." The teacher rips open the envelope. "Benny Morgenstern! Sorry, kids, it's the school's policy not to give out more than one A."

On the contrary! Every school wants to show off its collective success vis-à-vis other schools, and they want as many students as possible to get A's. There is no quota. There are no limitations. There is no competition! It's only our ego and competitive nature that generate competitive feelings with our classmates. No competition actually exists—no one will be crowned the winner.

Ask yourself what would satisfy you more: if you got a B in math and the rest of the class got C's and D's, or if you got an A in math and so did the rest of the class. Give it some deep and sincere thought.

In my Super Student Success seminars, most students will say that being the one getting the B will give them more satisfaction. In the words of one of them: "What's the fun if everyone gets an A?" I find this astonishing.

Here's another question: What's your purpose in school? What's your goal? Getting an A or getting a B? Why do you care what the others get?

Rule #3: Choose Your Green Times, and Don't Study During Red Times

Is there anyone among us who hasn't suffered a guilty conscience after sleeping late? Society has taught us that he who wakes up early for work and school is diligent. It also states that he who wakes up late is lazy, right?

Accordingly, I have no recollection of the classes that took place at 7:40 a.m. throughout my high school years. I always believed this problem was solely mine. But as time went by, I slowly discovered that there were other people who didn't like to wake up early in the morning. In fact, I was surprised to learn that this includes 80 percent of the population. I once read a scientific article that said, essentially, that there are morning people, those who like to wake up early and are more efficient in the morning, and then there are night people, those who are more efficient at night and like to wake up late.

Our memory's ability varies throughout the day and week. Each one of us has a "prime time" in which his brain works in the most efficient way and his memory is at its maximal strength. For example, my prime times are between 10:00 a.m. and noon, and then from 5:00 to 8:00 p.m. At these hours I feel that my ability to concentrate, as well as understand and memorize, are at their prime. This doesn't mean that the rest of the time I am mentally paralyzed. All it means is that during the times I mentioned, my capacity for learning is greater.

I have named these off and peak hours "red time" and "green time," respectively, since they are analogous to driving on a road with traffic lights. If we keep hitting red lights, the ride will be longer and more annoying. On the other hand, the same drive can be smooth as silk if we hit the lights at the right times, just when they're turning green. This faster and more enjoyable ride will positively affect our mood for the rest of the day.

Each one of you knows what your peak (green) times are and is well familiar with your off (red) times. Chances are that the green time of the early risers among you is around two hours after waking up. At the same time, the night owls among you will experience your green time in the evening (though not necessarily). There are many reasons for this, some of which are related to our biological cycle during the day, including body temperature, blood pressure, and so on.

Pay attention to the times when you feel at your prime and make use of them. Do all your studying and other mental and creative efforts (such as writing, reading, homework, etc.), during your green times. These are your peak hours, when your brain gives you a green light to go forward and take advantage of the smooth path ahead. On the other hand, during your red times, perform tasks that do not entail mental effort (such as filing, opening your mail, etc.). These are times at which your brain signals you to stop, and if you go forward, it will only be a bumpy road. Accordingly, set your school class schedule to be in sync with your green times as much as possible.

If you've already been dragged into the late-night hours, don't rise early! Continue sleeping and study when you wake up. You might have less time to study, but the efficiency of your learning will be doubled.

Learn how to ride your green wave. You've prepared a cup of coffee, sliced off a piece of cake, and have finally sat down to study during your green time. Don't start off by reading the required material. The use of your brain is similar to the use of any other muscle, which requires warming up before intensive use. For this reason, it's recommended that you begin with intellectual warm-up exercises. Pick up the newspaper and leaf through it leisurely. Focus on the stories that interest you. Ten minutes later, put the paper away and move on to the material you need to study. This transition won't be too drastic, as your brain has already entered a "learning mode" of sorts, allowing you to ease your way into the ocean of information before you.

As time passes, you'll probably feel that you're in a total learning groove. Your aim is to stay on this green wave, just like an experienced surfer's goal is to ride as long as possible on the ocean's wave. It makes no difference if this wave lasts for an hour or four hours. As long as you feel you are "surfing" safely on this wave and flowing with the learning material, continue doing so.

Behave just like a surfer, who won't purposely throw himself off a wave. Keep riding the momentum for as long as it's possible. Don't break the wave! Don't get up for an initiated break because you planned it ahead of time, or because an old *Seinfeld* episode just started and you really feel like watching it. This will rob you of valuable time in your efforts to catch a new wave. Keep studying until you feel your mind beginning to wander.

After being on the wave for some time, you might fall off it for reasons that aren't under your control, like a friend popping by to say hi or your phone ringing. Or the wave might simply evaporate, just as any wave eventually reaches the seashore and dissipates to a small rush of water. As far as we are concerned, such a fall is the breaking point of the extended learning session. This is when it's time to stop studying. Don't try to force yourself to continue; you'll just waste your time.

Know when to start something and when to finish it. That's one of the most poignant points in Ecclesiastes, a book in the Old Testament: "A time to plant and a time to uproot, a time for seeking and a time for losing, a time for keeping and a time for throwing away, a time for silence and a time for speaking," and so on.

If you're already working on something, stay with it until you finish it. The moment you're done, forget about it, as if it never existed. The transition must be absolute: A time to study and a time to stop.

Do you know one of the most important directives for Jews in the Torah? Keeping the Sabbath. "Remember the Sabbath and to keep it holy," as it says in Exodus. Throughout history, Jews have risked their lives to keep the Sabbath: to light the Shabbat candles, bake challah (the traditional braided bread that Jews eat on the Sabbath), and say the blessing over the wine—all hidden from their oppressors. The very existence of

Shabbat made every Jew remove himself from his daily labors and dedicate a twenty-five-hour period every week to God: to rest, to pray, to learn, and to dine at the Shabbat table with his family.

Why do I bring up the Sabbath? Because it encapsulates, more than anything else, a complete transition from work to rest. The list of what is and is not permitted on Shabbat is long and meticulous. It is forbidden to work. During this time one should aspire to speak of holy things, such as the Torah, and not of mundane issues. One should wear nice clothes. Why? In order to help a person forget his daily worries so he can focus instead on the sublime. It's a day to recharge and to cleanse the mind for spiritual well-being.

One of the highest values in Judaism is not work or study. It's *rest*.

So . . . take a *real* break. Don't think about your studies when you're not studying! Research has shown that taking breaks helps the brain process what was learned and assimilate the information into the memory.

Many think that the intensive study over an extended period is the way to learn new material, but actually, the complete opposite is true. New material is better absorbed in our memory if we take breaks, and if the break time increases between one "wave" and another. A good, restful break is a must. If you feel tired during the day or after your green time, go rest! Take a half-hour nap (or more, if you really need it), and your batteries will be recharged.

I am well aware that an afternoon nap is considered to be sinful, especially in our busy, industrious culture. So let me tell you a secret—Winston Churchill used to take afternoon naps while he was Britain's prime minister. He did so even during wartime! If he could do this while carrying a bit more responsibility on his shoulders than we carry, then surely we can catnap as well.

Rule #4: Study First Class, Not Coach

The time before finals, or when we have to submit term papers, is usually very stressful. Heartless teachers rob us of our freedom and make us work hard—very, very hard. The nerve!

"How about going to a movie tonight?" a friend asks us. We probably answer with a sigh: "No chance of that happening. This month I have six exams and two papers to turn in. No movies. No parties. No going out. No shopping. No life. I have to stay at home. I hardly even have time to breathe."

We sadly bid him good-bye, and as we daydream about sunbathing on the beach, we go back to sit at our desk. The house is completely silent and within minutes we start feeling claustrophobic and restless. At this stage we begin the "just two minutes" phase.

"I'll take a little break and grab something from the refrigerator. It will take only two minutes," we rationalize.

But we don't stop there.

"I'll just watch the news update on TV. It will take only ten minutes."

"I'll call Janet—I've got to hear what's going on outside in the real world. It will take only five minutes."

Only two minutes, only ten minutes, only five minutes . . . and the suffering continues. Where does the suffering and subsequent depression stem from? Many times, the root of the problem lies in the fact that we're in a self-imposed prison.

Who decided that it's necessary to study at home or in a quiet environment? Why should we "ground" ourselves and not go out at all?

We all know that each of us is different from everyone else. For this reason, it's impossible to conclude that silence is required for studying. There are those of us who really do need a quiet environment in order to concentrate, such as at the library or at home. Yet others find silence to be a disturbance to concentration. These people need soft background music or even loud rock music. Some people aren't able to study with others and prefer to shut themselves off alone. In contrast, some feel most efficient when they are surrounded by others studying together. The idea is to study in the most comfortable way for you. Think of this as your personal first-class environment.

I've always found it difficult to concentrate in quiet. Whenever I had to perform mental tasks, such as studying or writing, I always chose to do so in coffee shops, surrounded by people and with music at a normal volume playing in the background. Noise does disturb me. I cannot concentrate at extremely bustling coffee shops, where people have to compete with really loud music in order to be heard. In my ideal first-class environment, the coffee shop is smaller and less popular, with about five or six couples. These people are chatting at normal frequency, while the music is monotonous and pleasant. This is the only way I'm able to concentrate and produce something with good results.

In the book *Netivot Hochma*, a short kabbalistic text from the sixth century, it's written: "A man cannot learn in a place that his heart does not desire." Each person is responsible for finding the manner, situation, and time in which he is able to learn and remember best. For example, I once read about a Buddhist scholar who recommended studying near a river because it creates a serenity that aids the memory. A peaceful river, of course . . . I mean, if you're trying to learn on the banks of the Amazon River with a crocodile staring at your book and a jaguar peering over your shoulder to see what page you're on, that might be a bit distracting.

The bottom line is that only you know what's best for you. No one else will be able to tell you otherwise. Ignore those who sit at the library and seem to be efficient. They are different from you. Don't just sit and dream of a sunset, the sound of the ocean, and a piña colada with a little paper umbrella. Take your books and notebooks and go to the beach (or lake or stream) at sunset. If you're not near water, sit down at a coffee shop, order a coffee, and occasionally look up from your books to watch the sunset.

However—and this is important, regardless of where you decide to learn—hide from all others.

Rule #5: Hide

There's a secret button with an amazing function that cellular telephone companies don't tell you about. The reason you haven't heard about this button is because of its devastating impact on both human beings and cellular phone companies. It's called the on/off button, and it turns off the phone.

Shocking, isn't it? I know.

I too was shocked the first time I used this button. For more than ten minutes I couldn't call anyone and no one could contact me. I still have goose bumps when I recall the feeling—it was kind of like cutting off a part of my body.

The good news is that after you practice turning off the phone a few times, you learn how to breathe normally and, miraculously, you eventually get used to it.

I'm now at level four, meaning I can keep my phone shut off for four hours! (Level one is five minutes. The masters reach level 10—these are divine beings who can live without cell phones and the Internet altogether, such as monks, nuns, and Amish senior citizens.) The point being, if you manage to keep your phone off for four hours, something incredible will happen—you won't get calls for four hours, no one will bother you, no one will distract you, and you will study efficiently! You will also discover that the world has not collapsed while you were disconnected.

> "For him who has conquered the mind, the mind is the best of friends; but for one who has failed to do so, his mind will remain the greatest enemy."
> —BHAGAVAD GITA

Becoming the unreachable student gives you great power. It's liberating that with all the advanced communication tools available, you cannot be reached! You are alone, with no interference, no distraction . . . it's only you and your books. You can't imagine how much you can get done when that phone is off.

Imagine our surfer catching a great wave. Fully focused and in total control, suddenly he hears a ringing sound . . . and it's coming from his waterproof cell phone, attached to his belt.

Jenny: "Mitch, where the heck are you? What's that roaring, windy sound?"

Mitch (shouting): "I'm surfing, baby. Caught the greatest wave ever!"

Jenny: "Did you see my birth control pills? I forgot to take them this week. . . ."

Splash. Mitch falls off his board into the ocean. He became distracted and lost his concentration and balance.

Here's some disturbing news. If you are riding your green wave in full concentration and your cell phone suddenly rings and you talk for only five minutes, it will take you fifteen minutes to reach the same level of concentration you had before the call. Once you realize this fact, you can understand how crucial it is to eliminate distraction.

In addition, eliminate other things that may make you feel uncomfortable. Free yourself from all distractions. If you're hot, turn on the air conditioner. Make some coffee ahead of time and eat something if you're hungry, which will help you focus better. Turn off the TV, lock the door, go offline. To make a long story short, become unreachable.

Rule # 6: Take Your Superman Pill

Each of us has one of these Superman pills. I'm talking about our secret motivators and sources of inspiration.

I learned this from my good friend Martin, when I was studying at the College of Europe in Belgium. Martin would always arrive for exams wearing a high-end tailor-made suit, fancy shirt, expensive tie, and . . . shorts and sandals.

"Why are you dressed up like this?" we'd ask between giggles.

"These are my lucky clothes," Martin would explain. "They make me feel special and if I feel special, my exam will be special."

Do you have a lucky shirt or a lucky pen? Use it to generate confidence.

Does a little Buddha or icon make you feel protected? Bring it to the exam.

Does praying make you stronger? Then pray. Prayer can help you concentrate. Pray to your inner strength, to faith in yourself. Prayer is a declaration of intention. In Judaism, for every deed and action there is a designated prayer. Before eating a meal with bread, Jews are commanded to wash their hands and say a blessing. Before venturing out on a journey, they recite the traveler's prayer. Before going to bed, they say the Shema. The purpose of these prayers is to help focus on the task at hand. Prayers are supposed to divert your attention from other things so you can concentrate on what you're about to do. They say: "I will focus all my attention on the path upon which I am now traveling, or the food that is before me." Such focusing aids in digestion, enhances awareness when driving, and, relevant to our discussion, boosts the level of effectiveness when studying.

You can invent your own prayer or personal mantra, a catchphrase you really believe in that will give you some kind of joy or motivation to begin whatever it is you set out to do.

So put on your personal Superman outfit for the exam, take out your favorite pen, place a lucky charm on the desk, write *B'H* (an acronym for the Hebrew phrase *b'ezrat hashem*, or "by the grace of God") on your notes, and pray. It's guaranteed to help—psychologically and spiritually.

Rule # 7: Become Intimate with Your Teacher

Well, not *that* way! That's rarely a good idea, especially if you're twelve years old and your teacher is seventy-four. Let me explain myself better.

Contrary to popular belief, teachers are human beings just like me and you. What this means is that they actually have feelings. They can feel joy, they can feel pain, and some even feel compassion. New research even indicates that they have a social life outside of school. What this means is that many take your success or failure personally. So what can you do?

For one thing, show up to class. Woody Allen said that 80 percent of success is just showing up. In fact, teachers take it personally if you don't show up, especially the really boring teachers. They realize that they're boring but believe that you haven't noticed this shortcoming. If you don't show up to class, however, it will hit them: "Oh, he noticed I'm boring . . . he doesn't enjoy my lectures. That really hurts my feelings—I guess I'll have to flunk him."

Excuses for skipping class are unacceptable—not even "I was sick" or "My thumb hurts." Actually, the following are the only valid excuses worth trying out:

> "I have to prepare for my interviews with Oprah and Dr. Phil."

> "I got stuck in Moscow because the pilot didn't show up."

> "The class is based on a book I wrote."

There's no doubt that a good teacher can do wonders. A gifted teacher or lecturer who relays information in an interesting and dynamic manner will significantly influence your ability to remember what is being taught. The problem arises, of course, with those classes in which the lecturer or subject doesn't interest you and you just sit and count the minutes until the bell rings. Simple principles can help you get the most out of every lecture, which will help you to better remember what is being said.

First, as mentioned, make the lecture interesting for yourself. Find the points of interest in the lecturer's words; ask the lecturer questions.

In addition to this, imagine yourself sitting in class alone while the lecturer is talking only to you. The idea of being solo will heighten your willingness to absorb what is said.

Sit in the front of the lecture hall. There's a huge difference in one's ability to absorb information and concentrate during lectures between those who sit in the front and those who sit in the back. The students who sit in the back tend to cut themselves off from what's going on in class faster than the students who sit in the front. As a result, the ones in the front are more involved in the class, and their ability to focus and remember the lecturer's words is greater.

Don't take thorough notes during the lecture. It's shocking, I know. Still, there's no way around it. It just isn't possible to follow the lecturer while writing down everything she's saying at the same time. This is simply an impossible mission! We're talking about two contradicting activities. Listening is passive, while writing is active. We're trying to both internalize information and externalize it immediately. It's true that this is what we're taught to do, and by the time we hit college, we've honed our ability to write down most of what the lecturer says. But honestly, how many times have you given up while trying to record the lecture, hoping you can fill in the blanks from a friend's notes? How many times have you tripped yourself up by missing a word or two, and before you know it, you have no idea what was said?

The reason for all this is simple. It just isn't possible to do two things at the same time and do both well. The faster the lecturer talks, the more the pressure grows. The lecture ends up turning into a wild-goose chase of sorts, where the words take on a certain holiness, as if God is saying them Himself, and if you miss a word, you miss enlightenment.

Now please, calm down. True, what the lecturer says is important, but it's not everything. We miss the purpose of the lecture—to listen. The point isn't to summarize, but to attend. If the lecturer is interesting, it would be much more enjoyable to set down your pen, lean back, and listen to the lecture. If the lecturer is exceptionally fascinating, something amazing usually happens: without even noticing, we stop writing and get caught up in what she's saying. Why? Because it's much more meaningful—and fun—to listen and be involved in a captivating class than to scribble away, which only helps to pass the time. The process of summarizing the lecture doesn't allow us to absorb the material and to remember it.

So, you may ask, what's the solution?

During the lecture itself, sit in the front of the hall or classroom. Sit comfortably and listen without the pressure to write down all that's being said. Be involved. And most important, enjoy the lecture, for this is the purpose of our studies. You may write key points of interest for future reference, but don't try to catch up and summarize every sentence that you hear.

If your instructor is someone who expects you to remember *everything* she says, and will test you on it, use a recorder to tape the class instead of trying to write everything down.

Rule # 8: Don't Be Perfect

I received a phone call one morning from my daughter's fifth-grade teacher: "Your daughter fainted during physical education. Please come pick her up from the nurse's room at school."

I rushed to school and escorted my daughter to the car.

"What happened?" I asked, worried.

She described her difficulty running two laps around the schoolyard. After several additional questions and clarifications, she confessed: "And I didn't want to come in last."

We continued talking about nutrition, getting in shape and, more important, about "pride and prejudice."

"In your next phys ed class," I said, "there's a very difficult task I want to give you. Are you willing to take the challenge?"

"Yes," she replied, more curious than willing.

"Your mission is to run the first lap, walk the second lap, and come in last. If you don't come in last, your mission will have failed." I smiled. "Can you do that?"

She was amused but also clearly felt uncomfortable. "Yes. I'll try," she said.

What do you prefer: being a successful student with the highest grades or a success in your life?

Isn't the answer obvious? You'd prefer to be a success in your life.

If this is the case, don't try to be in the top 5 percent of your class. Try to be a good student—just not the best student. Why? For two reasons:

1. There's no absolute correlation between success in school and success in careers. In fact, studies have shown that those who receive the highest grades in school usually don't reach the top level of their companies. They get stuck somewhere in the middle. Top executives usually had average grades. It makes sense—to reach the top you need social skills and you need to be a good communicator. When you devote all your time to just studying, by definition, you interact less with others.
2. Aspiring to be at the top of your class may be very distressing and create the opposite result. It can become an obsession for some, and as with other obsessions, things can get blown out of proportion. You'll review the material ten times when three or four times would have been enough; you'll spend two weeks studying for an exam when three days would have been enough; and so forth.

Do you know the best book that was ever written? Well, it's still being written because it needs *just* a little bit more editing, *just* some tiny little improvements, *just* one superfast review . . . There will always be *one* more thing to do, add, or change to make it the best.

It never ends for certain people! Are you one of them? Trying to be perfect creates anxiety and stress. Don't try to be the perfect student; try to be a good student. Don't try to be number one in your class; try to be number eight. And something surprising just might happen—you might become the best!

When you try to be good enough, you reduce anxiety, you're not obsessing to prove anything, and you don't suffer from unnecessary pressure. It's much easier to succeed when you take things easy, in a way that allows you to enjoy what you're learning.

And yes, I realize there are parents who are reading this who will say, "Well, my problem is exactly the opposite. My son [or daughter] is far from being a perfectionist! He's lazy and isn't making any effort at all!" It's okay. Tell kids like that they can remain lazy and invest less effort in school. Give them this book and mention it was written by someone just like them. Tell them there is a surprise inside and all they have to do is read this chapter and then the next one, because now we'll learn the greatest secret of them all: how to cheat on exams without getting caught.

I'm talking legally, of course. We'll use memory tricks to remember twice the amount of material in half the time it would normally take.

~~~~~~

CHAPTER 15

TWICE AS MUCH IN HALF THE TIME

The Magical Guide to Successful Studying

IN REAL LIFE, I ASSURE YOU, THERE IS
NO SUCH THING AS ALGEBRA.
—*Fran Lebowitz*

WHEN WAS THE last time you had to calculate how long it would take you to fill a bathtub if two Indians left Tallahassee at 7:00 a.m., riding their horses at an average speed of 47 mph during the windy season, while eating a seven-inch country-style gefilte fish loaf that costs $4 an inch and was heated to an exact temperature of 80 degrees?

My teacher once asked me a similar question. I stood up, and as I left the classroom I said, "I'll be out here, Ms. Brown. Just call me back the minute the bath is completely full."

Okay, I'm kidding. Algebra does have its advantages.

Seriously, in mathematically oriented subjects, such as calculus, physics, economics, and computer programming, exams are based more on comprehension than on memory skills. When you prepare for such exams, you need to fully understand the different types of solutions and how to arrive at them by using one kind of formula or another. There's no need to memorize great amounts of material; the key here is to practice, as the emphasis is on logic.

For our intents and purposes, we'll focus on the kind of exam that calls for memorizing inhumane amounts of information. So let's sit down and study together.

Exam season has arrived. Our desk is adorned with five books, ten papers, and twenty lecture summaries. How are we going to conquer all of this? As with any journey, let's take it one step at a time.

Do you recall ever going on a hiking trip where, after a few hours, the guide points at a distant mountain and says, "That's where the buses will be waiting"? The mountain seems to be about ten miles away. Our first thought is, "No way! We have to walk *all* the way over there? Funny joke!" Still, we keep on walking until we finally reach the mountain, because there's no other choice. It's the same with the material we need to remember; while the end seems to be nowhere in sight, with perseverance, we'll make it.

GOOD BEGINNINGS ARE INTERESTING BEGINNINGS

Start with something simple and interesting. Begin with your study session by reading something enjoyable, like a newspaper article, a book of short stories, the IRS annual board meeting minutes, the ingredients on a Froot Loops cereal box—anything that intrigues you, really. As I've said, the brain, like any other muscle, needs to ease into its workout.

You wouldn't start sprinting the moment you roll out of bed in the morning, and in the winter a car's motor needs to warm up before it's driven. Take about ten or fifteen minutes to get going, and then move on to whatever it is you need to study for class.

FAMILIARIZE YOURSELF WITH THE FAMILIAR

It's very important that you fully understand the content of difficult and complicated material. The Talmud teaches, "One who comprehends his Talmud—does not forget it easily."

"Isn't that rather obvious?" you may ask.

Not necessarily. There are some things that seem blatantly apparent, meaning we think we understand, but in reality we might be missing something. I'll give you an example. I'm sure that you've heard the expressions *ad hoc*, *modus vivendi*, *tabula rasa*, and *bona fide*. "What does *ad hoc* mean?" I'll ask in my seminars. "What's the translation, literally?"

Here's a typical response: "It's . . . um . . . well . . . I mean . . . that is . . . I believe . . . I guess . . . it's probably . . . a kind of . . . past event, maybe? Or maybe not."

"And how about *modus vivendi*?" I continue.

"That has something to do with a new fashion module for measuring?" someone once suggested.

We've all heard these phrases, but the truth is we never took the time to look up their exact meanings.

Here are some additional humorous "misknowledgeables" that children wrote on exams:

> H_2O is hot water and CO_2 is cold water.
> The ancient Egyptians were mummies who wrote in hydraulics.
> The inhabitants of Moscow are called Mosquitos.

A gladiator is something that keeps a room warm.

A vacuum is a large, empty space where the Pope lives.

Electric volts are named after Voltaire, who invented electricity.

I'm not sure how clouds get formed, but the clouds know how to do it, and that is the important thing.

Be sure you understand what you learn. It's almost impossible for the human brain to remember things that do not make sense or are unclear.

And don't give up too easily. Take an extra minute or two. Invest a little bit of extra energy to make sure that you understand it all. Sometimes, if you don't get the first part of something, everything else that you learn afterward won't make sense. It's like a necklace. If the first link is weak, the whole chain is affected.

IDENTIFY THE CREAM OF THE CROP

The *Tao Te Ching*, the classic text of Chinese philosophy traditionally believed to be written by Lao Tzu around the sixth century B.C., presents a way of life intended to restore harmony to a kingdom racked by disorder. Here are two of its central points:

> Thirty spokes share the wheel's hub; it is the center hole that makes it useful.

> More words count less. Hold fast to the center.

Learning materials such as books, papers, and summaries are like a landscape. When you view a landscape there will always be a lot of things to see but few central objects that stand out and catch your eye. These may be a mountaintop, a red-roofed house, a stream, or a large tree. They're what end up seared into your memory. If asked to share what you've seen, you'll probably mention those very objects that stood out. It is neither necessary nor important to remember all the details. Each piece of information that you wish to retain should be divided into sections, with the most important word or phrase noted at the beginning—and make it a word you can imagine. The memory resembles a fishing net: only the big fish will get caught, and the smaller fish will always escape through the net's holes.

Three times a week, in synagogues across the globe, the weekly portion of the Torah is read. Each portion is titled with a key word that describes the main theme. The Hebrew name for Genesis is taken from the word of the first paragraph of the first book of the Torah, *bereshit* (in the beginning): "In the beginning, God created the heaven and the earth." "These are the generations of Noah," begins the portion of Noah. And the next portion is *lech lecha* (get thee out): "Now the Lord said to Avram, 'Get thee out,'" and so on.

Noah, for example, conjures up the image of an old man boarding an ark with pairs of animals trailing behind him, right? "Get thee out" is a phrase that stimulates the imagination because it actually calls for physically changing locales. Key words need to be eye-catching, as we've already mentioned—they're like landmarks.

Now, please read the following article. Try to read it in one sitting; however, at first ignore the highlighted words. Read it as though you're reading an editorial in a daily newspaper. Treat it as a text that you aren't obligated to read but which you choose to read out of interest. After you finish reading it, go over it again quickly, paying attention to the highlighted words. These are the key words that actually constitute the topic or main idea described in the given section.

FUTURE PROFESSIONS: THE HUMAN FACTOR

E. Katz

"The professions which were necessary in the past will vanish in the future because of the computer's ability to replace man," argues Dr. Carl **Bernard**. He explains his reasoning as he describes the expected outcomes of the information revolution in which we are living. "People will order airline tickets via the **Internet**. This is where they will be able to receive detailed information and plan their desired journey. By doing so, there will be no need for travel agents. The same is true regarding insurance agents."

As someone who was once employed in the tourism industry, I disagree with this assumption.

Let's take, for instance, a person in the market to buy a **house**. Today, all he has to do is open the newspaper or go online to find all the information he needs. According to Dr. Bernard's theory, it's only natural that an occupation such as a real estate agent would vanish. But in reality, real estate agencies are still very much thriving.

The **abundance** of information bombarding us today is exactly why we still have a deep need for the human factor. It's no coincidence that our indulged society has brought on the **flourishing** of coaches and experts whose sole purpose is to help people find their way to the essence of matters. This is the case with a real estate agent, whose duty is to channel the buyer's desire toward the yearned-for house.

Today, someone who dreams about a trip through the south of **France** is able to receive all the information he could want on the Internet. This information usually includes all the attractions, hotels, and restaurants in the area. He is able to access instant prices and see breathtaking photos of each and every site. But this magnificent information bank pales in comparison to the professional opinion of a travel agent. A recommendation such as "Trust me, stay at the X hotel. It's quiet, clean, offers great service, and a delicious breakfast. Much better than the W" will have greater impact than the impersonal information network. Our traveler will appreciate the peace of mind—based on personal recommendation—that he is indeed headed to the right place. Besides, if the trip turns out to be a disappointment, whom will he turn to in order to complain? The World Wide Web?

Swissair customarily conducts educational tours for travel agents, as do many other companies. At their own expense, they'll treat a group of around thirty travel agents to business-class air travel. The company will arrange accommodations at the most luxurious hotels, wine and dine them at top restaurants, and pamper them throughout their trip. The company is highly aware of the fact that the travel agent has significant influence over the decision of which airline her customers should choose for their trips.

In the convention field, **videoconferencing** has changed the way people meet. Today, a lecturer at a university is able to sit in a conference room together with seven other scientists. At the same time, he is able to conduct a videoconference with three other groups of scientists in England, Germany, and Japan. Imagine the financial savings involved here. No need for flights, hotels, and the actual organization of the conference—a monumental and expensive task.

Yet, in actuality, that lecturer and those scientists would rather go somewhere where they could meet in person. No technology will be able to replicate the experience of gathering and socializing with their colleagues from around the world. There will never be a substitute for direct human contact.

And by the way, who will take care of the arrangements to get them to the conference? Right, the travel agents. So the human factor will continue to lead, direct, and determine any future occupations and work markets. An abundance of information and advanced technology will bring about only greater employment. In 1973, **E. Bluestone** wrote, "Technology has given meaning to the lives of many **technicians**." He foresaw that there is truly no replacement for the direct connection between men.

In every paragraph of the above article, a word or two was highlighted. These key words were chosen to represent the general idea described in that paragraph. Let's look at these highlighted words and describe what lies behind them in a few words:

Bernard and **Internet.** The name of the person quoted is Bernard; it is his theory that inspired the writing of the article. The purpose of the article, as mentioned, was to refute his claim that the Internet will replace man.

House. This word reminds us that a person is able to make use of any resource concerning the kind of house he is searching for. As a result of this "reality," the real estate agents who do exist are supposedly unneeded.

Abundance and **flourishing.** The abundance of confusing information has brought about the flourishing of human consultants.

France. An example of the power and influence a travel agent wields when a client is planning a trip abroad (travel to France, in this example).

Swissair. The Swiss airline is one of many that conduct agent tours. This fact strengthens the article's counter-arguments. In spite of their tremendous advertising budget, airlines prefer to invest in human resources. They too believe that as a result of this investment, the agent who will recommend their airline to a client will yield more influence than an ad in the Sunday paper.

Videoconferencing. In spite of the advantages of a conference conducted via video link, the shortcomings of this type of meeting are evident. They stem from our innate need for human contact.

Bluestone and **technicians.** A humoristic example of the inevitable connection between technology and technicians.

Now, after understanding what every word reminds us of in a specific paragraph, we have several options—and we've learned the first two:

1. Connect the words and create a chain where each word reminds us of the next one.
2. Create a file—think about a certain room in our home and link each key word to one of the items on our home list.
3. Craft an associative story using the key words.

In Chapter 5 we demonstrated how to create an associative story with eels, oranges, and Mercedes cars. Let's do so now with the "real deal." We're going to create a connection between the key words and make up a humorous story.

Let's imagine a big, lovable St. Bernard dog. A personal computer (representing the Internet) is tied to its collar, in place of the usual wine barrel. The dog is about to buy a house, with the hopes of trading the computer for the house. The house's backyard is barren, and the dog wishes it had an abundance of flowers so he could, ahem, "water" them. So the dog decides to take a trip to France, where he can collect ideas of how a backyard should really look. He chooses to fly Swissair, since he's a Swiss dog. In France, he feels lonely. So he holds videoconferences with his family and friends twice a day. When the dog finally returns home, he brings his girlfriend a robot as a gift, courtesy of the robot technicians he met in Lyon. The robot is adorned with blue stones that sparkle in the dark.

The associative story must be strong and clear in your mind. In order to remember it in the most efficient way, ask yourself guiding questions: Why does the Saint Bernard have a computer hanging from its collar? Because he's going to try to trade it in for a house. What didn't he like about the house? The backyard was barren and he wished it had an abundance of flowers. What did he do in France? Nothing.

He was lonely, so he held videoconferences with friends and family. What special gift did he bring back upon his return home? A robot (courtesy of the technicians) decorated with blue stones.

In order to remember what this story is connected to, associate between the first key word in the story, *(St.) Bernard*, and the title of the article, "Future Professions—The Human Factor." Imagine that one day St. Bernard dogs will try to replace us in certain professions.

Now put this subject aside. Let's go back to how we can remember material for an upcoming exam by using a different method. Say that you're taking a course in political science or economics and you have to remember the budget system of your typical European country.

This is what the budget breakdown looks like:

STATE BUDGET

CASH FLOW BUDGET

Expenses	Revenues
Government offices	Direct taxes
Subsidies	Indirect taxes
Transfer payments	Internal loans
Loan returns	Licenses

We can see that the budget is divided into two parts:

Cash flow budget—revenues
Cash flow budget—expenses

Using the Roman room method, let's decide to link everything related to the cash flow budget in the two rooms that deal with "flows" (think water): the bathroom and the laundry room. The file (room) where we will hang the various components of the cash flow budget revenues will be the bathroom, for this purpose.

Imagine a sign hanging on the bathroom door that says INCOME (this is the door through which we enter the bathroom). Now, let's choose four items in the bathroom that will be used as hangers on which the four components of the cash flow budget revenues will be hung.

The bathroom list includes:

Shower
Bath
Towels
Toilet

As we learned previously, we'll take the first component of the state budget revenues, direct taxes, and connect it to the shower, our first item.

Using the word-resemblance method, "direct taxes" may become *directions to Texas*. We may imagine our shower curtain covered with a map of the southern United States. Instead of water, arrows are streaming out of the shower head, splashing all over.

The second component of our revenues is "indirect taxes." *Indirect* will become *Indian*, which we'll connect with the second item, the bath. Imagine an Indian chief lying in a warm bubble bath, his feathers dripping water, blended with arrows shooting out of the showerhead.

"Internal loans," the third revenue component, will become *Interpol*. The third item is towels. Let's imagine that a man is standing in your bathroom. This man has a police cap on his head with INTERPOL in large red letters embroidered on it, and a large towel wrapped around his waist.

The fourth component is licenses. You don't even have to change this into another word that sounds similar. The fourth hanger is the toilet. Imagine that you are sitting on the toilet when suddenly the Interpol agent asks to see your license for using the toilet! In the past, people were free to do so at their own will, but no more. From now on, you need a special license to use the toilet.

> Never, never, never, never, *ever, ever* repeat things. This, of course, is a joke. But there's no getting around it. Repetition is one of the most important elements in remembering things over the long term. In the Talmud's Tractate Sanhedrin, it is written, "Every learner of Torah who does not review it is like a man who sows seeds but doesn't harvest the crop." Everything learned must be recited again and again.

We've now learned how to remember the components of the cash flow budget revenues for an average European country. But to actually remember them, you need repetition.

Only by repeatedly going over something will it stay in your head. If you don't review the material, you won't retain it, and if you don't remember it, then you have wasted your time and energy.

Efficient repetition methods include discussions and question-and-answer sessions. These are made more effective by repeating the process five times. If you are studying alone, try doing it aloud while singing. "Anyone reading without a tune and reciting without a song—sentences will not come alive for him," it is said in the Talmud. "He who studies in song will remember better."

It's not only the singing as a technique that helps the memory, but also the music itself. Try it out. Study with a tune. Hum Frank Sinatra's "Strangers in the Night," adding the text you need to learn. "Di-rec-tions to Texas . . . I need to pay my taxes, internal loans . . . the Interpol agent will come and take me . . . la la la . . ."

Another technique is to walk and talk. "Why do Jews study while swaying and pacing back and forth?" a Chinese diplomat once asked me. That's the same question that the king of the Khazars asked Rabbi Yehuda Halevi. In his twelfth-century book *The Kuzari*, Rabbi Halevi explains what was scientifically confirmed years later: that the swaying keeps the body warm and increases blood flow.

Did you ever study while pacing back and forth? If so, you did good. Movement works better for the memory because it improves one's ability to think and learn. In other words, it's preferable to study while standing up or walking. The swaying establishes a certain rhythm that helps you concentrate, and it also increases oxygen flow to the brain. This extra oxygen enhances your ability to think more clearly.

If you think that I'm saying that the brain gets less oxygen when the body sits, you're right. And it's not only when you're sitting. The amount of oxygen in the air has decreased over the last few hundred years because of pollution. Today the amount of pure oxygen in the air in the downtown area of your average city is about 21 percent, compared to the higher percent it used to be at the beginning of the twentieth century. That's the reason why so many city slickers suffer from migraines, allergies, drowsiness, and other ailments. All these affect one's ability to concentrate and be alert. In order to think more effectively, an increase in blood flow to the brain needs to occur, which brings more oxygen to the brain. A great way to achieve this is by walking, rocking back and forth, and swimming. Some people even suggest doing headstands before studying.

Did you know that Einstein conceived the theory of

relativity while he was taking a walk? And that Victor Hugo wrote *Les Misérables* while standing up? Mozart composed many pieces while walking around. And Beethoven would pour ice water over his head before he sat down to compose in order to increase his attention level.

Rehearse and repeat your associations for the exam while walking about a room, in the park, or in the street. When you finish, forget all about it. It's sealed in your brain. Now you're ready for the exam. Good luck!

THE DAY OF THE EXAM

Yes, the day of the exam always eventually arrives. We are anxious, and this is natural. We sit in a quiet classroom. We are surrounded by dozens of students who may have studied more hours than we have, yet we aren't stressed. This is because we have mastered the material. We'll be able to *perfectly* answer any question concerning the subject we have studied.

Notice that the subject of the exam doesn't really matter. There is always just one question: what are the five items that appear in every room in our house?

This is the only thing we have to remember. All of the rest of the facts can be remembered from these items through an associative link. We will be able to extract these facts in record time.

The exam sheet is passed out, and one lands on our desk. We look at it, and see that there are two questions:

1. In the future, will professions that are necessary today vanish following the Internet's ability to replace manpower? Provide reasons, arguments, explanations, descriptions, illustrations, and poems.

2. What are the components which make up the typical European country's budget? Short answers only.

We smile and begin the "copying process"—transferring the information from our memory onto the exam sheet.

Question 1: The Future Professions = St. Bernard

Let's reconstruct our associative story, and write down the key words on the side, for the heck of it. "Hmm . . . Bernard—computer/Internet."

ANSWER #1

Dr. Carl Bernard argued that occupations that were once necessary will vanish as a result of the Internet's ability to replace manpower . . .

"Let's think now, what did the dog do with the computer? Buy a house, that's it!"

A person who buys a house is able to use any information bank he wishes to, but still, there are many real estate agents . . .

"What happened to the dog? He wished the house's backyard had an abundance of flowers where he could pee to his heart's content."

The abundance of information has brought on the flourishing of coaches and experts whose sole purpose is . . .

"What did the dog decide to do? Take a trip to France."

But this magnificent information bank pales in comparison to the professional opinion of a travel agent . . .

"How did the dog get to France? He flew on Swissair."
   Swissair is an example of . . .

"What happened in France? In France, the dog felt really lonely, because he's Swiss. So he held videoconferences with his family and friends."
   In the convention field, videoconferencing has changed the way people meet. . . . Yet there will never be a substitute for direct human contact.

"When the dog returned, he brought back a robot purchased from technicians, adorned with sparkling blue stones."
   The human factor . . . as E. Bluestone wrote, "Technology has given meaning . . ."

We are done with the first question. Writing it out took exactly fifteen minutes. We're anxious to answer the second question. We really want to prove to the world how great our memory is!

Question 2: The Typical European Country's Budget
This is no problem whatsoever. "Cash flow budget . . . let's see. Flows, water—the bathroom and the laundry room," you say to yourself.
   "Revenues. First item, shower—directions to Texas. That's **direct taxes.**
   "Second item, the bath—Indian. That's **indirect taxes.**
   "Third item, towels—the Interpol agent wearing a towel. That's **internal loans.**
   "Fourth item, toilet—the Interpol agent asks for your license. **Licenses.**"
   See how easy it is to remember all this creatively instead of repetitively memorizing it in an illogical and inefficient way?
   "This is all fine and dandy when we're dealing with two

articles," you're probably thinking to yourself. "But remembering ten books?"

Please allow me to remind you of two points I have stressed earlier in this book.

1. There is no limit to your memory's capacity. Ten books may seem like a lot, but if you think about it, you'll have to store all the material for the exam in your memory one way or another! You'll do so whether you're dealing with two books and five articles or twenty books and forty articles. This is what's required of you in order to pass the exam, and you'll do it. The only question now is, do you want to do it the hard, boring way, or the easy and interesting way? You've just learned the techniques. The choice is yours.

2. Trust your memory. The basic instinct, as we've seen, is to flinch away from this method: "My brain isn't used to working in such a way"; "This is just too difficult," "It's better to just stick with the tried and true." The only doubt here is your own doubt. Yes, it takes a little practice until it becomes second nature, but mastering it will eventually save you time and greatly reduce the amount of reviewing required of you.

You have my word that by using this new method you will be able to study *twice the material in half the time*. Take it step by step. Soon you will discover how quickly and efficiently you are able to remember anything your heart desires. There is no limit to the key words and associative links that you are able to remember for an exam. Try just one chapter, and then add another. You will quickly discover that your brain can no longer work any other way.

You are also welcome to try out the Roman Room software I created for students at www.smart-memory.com.

My personal summaries for exams were made up of lists of hundreds of key words that served to jog my memory on anything I wished to write about. The following document is the translation of a review for an exam I took in public management. I wrote down these key words on the questionnaire of the exam itself. The key words listed here cover close to 150 pages of the main subjects and points! Of course, most of these words will mean nothing to you. But for me, every word was a seed that sprouted a description of three to ten lines on the exam sheet.

This is the original questionnaire:

THE FACULTY OF POLITICAL SCIENCE

**Final exam for "Introduction to Public Management"—
Makeup Exam, 2/23/1989
This exam consist of two parts.
The time allowed for each part is two hours.**

Part Two

Please write about two of the following subjects, using the material taught in class, according to your own understanding:

(It's possible to receive up to 35 points for every question in this section.)

Question 1: Main models of organizations.
Question 2: Politics and management.
Question 3: Why are reforms required for management and what is keeping them from being performed in the State of New York?

POL' AND MANAG'		REFORMS	NEW YORK
Pizza	Good	Refineries	Roads
Golf	Gong	Music	Design
Memory	God	Diamond	Rigid
Italy	Gambling	Bonus	Conservative
Ointment	Shooting Range	New York	Need

POL' AND MANAG'		REFORMS	NEW YORK
Monkey	Monkey	Hammer	Power
Glasses	Carrier	Strategy	Performing
Normative Care	Kosher	Citizen	Consent
Innovation	Outdoors	Bed	
Research and Development	Edited	Sleep	
White House	Mechanism	Computer	
Neck tie		Chair	
Labor		Public	
Tree		Recommendations	

Don't be fearful about failing an exam or a class. The world is full of people who failed exams, were expelled from school, or quit on their own. Not only did this not matter, it sometimes even contributed to their future success. Some famous examples include Albert Einstein, who failed the entrance exams to the Polytechnic Institute of Zurich; Thomas Edison, who dropped out of school and was educated by his mother at home; and Abraham Lincoln, who studied law on his own since no school would accept him. Each one of them found a learning path that worked for them and contributed to their future success.

"One day, I went to take a business management course at a university," recounts a famous businessman who had no formal education yet became one of the world's richest people. "The course was fascinating. It was there that I learned how to do business 'correctly,'" he continues. "Very soon afterward I turned from a billionaire into a millionaire."

Keep things in proportion, and make learning a fun and positive experience.

CHAPTER 16

MASTERING THE CEREMONY

A Super Memory for Presentations

OSCAR AND FRED ARE SITTING ON A BENCH.
"WHAT WOULD YOU LIKE PEOPLE TO SAY ABOUT YOU
AT YOUR FUNERAL?" ASKS OSCAR.
FRED REPLIES, "I WOULD LIKE THEM TO POINT AT MY
BODY AND CRY OUT EXCITEDLY: 'LOOK! HE *MOVED*!'"

DURING ONE OF his comedy routines, Jerry Seinfeld talked about an American survey that asked people what they are most afraid of. Ninety-eight percent replied that public speaking scared them the most. The rest opted for death.

What this means, according to Seinfeld, is that when it comes to being at a funeral, most people would prefer being the deceased to being the one giving the eulogy.

Public speaking is a very important skill that I think

everyone should acquire. It's needed in every aspect of life in order to communicate effectively and to convince gorgeous men or women to date you.

It was in ancient Greece and Rome that great orators brought the world such renowned works as *Rhetorica ad Herennium*, one of the oldest Latin texts on rhetoric and persuasion (author unknown), Cicero's *De Oratore*, and Aristotle's *Rhetoric*. However, one of the most substantial and impressive works on the subject belongs to Marcus Fabius Quintilianus, a Roman rhetorician from Hispania and author of *Institutio Oratoria*, a monumental work comprising twelve volumes. Quintilianus organized the discipline of oratory into five canons: *inventio* (discovery of arguments), *dispositio* (arrangement of arguments), *elocutio* (expression or style), *memoria* (memorization), and *pronuntiatio* (delivery). In this chapter, we shall learn how to smoothly deliver a presentation according to the Roman's method, concentrating on *memoria* and *pronuntiatio*.

The main cause of the fear of public speaking is . . . well . . . the public. Actually, what's scary about the prospect of talking in front of an audience is the possibility of suddenly forgetting what we wanted to say, as hundreds of eyes stare at us. The best way to counter such a fear is to *not* memorize a speech. If you do, one of two things might happen: (1) you might forget one word, and as a result of this, you might forget all the following words, or (2) you might worry so much about forgetting a specific word that it could bring about a blackout, which is basically paralysis of your memory.

Before we learn how to remember what we want to say, let me emphasize three important points which will save you time, sweat, and tears.

Point #1: There are probably countless subjects you would

like to talk about: convincing sales arguments, fascinating facts, amusing anecdotes, and so on. The natural tendency is to mention them all. Whether you're presenting your company's finest product or lecturing to student chefs about marinated mosquito knees—a new and revolutionary dish you've artfully invented—please remember that the audience isn't interested in hearing every little detail. The audience only wants to hear what's relevant.

Point #2: Sales presentations, acknowledgments, and speeches by the master of ceremonies should last for only a few minutes, and no more than fifteen. After eight minutes, the audience will stop pondering about the wonders of your lecture and start dreaming about the benefits of a strong cup of coffee. During Quintilianus's days, speeches tended to be long and embellished (well, you know, there was nothing better to do back then but listen to speeches). Even so, Quintilianus advocated for simple and clear communication with an emphasis on short messages. Study sessions and other lectures should last for no more than forty-five minutes. Every student's concentration and absorption capacity approaches zero after three-quarters of an hour. You'll discover that even if you try to surprise them with exotic acrobatics, no one will take any interest in what you're saying from forty-six minutes on. For any type of presentation, plan ahead. What is the main point you'd like to convey? Decide upon the three or four main issues that will achieve the purpose of your presentation or lecture and create the impression you seek.

Point #3: Prior to writing down and organizing the information which you are interested in conveying, keep in mind that the audience will only remember the following:

- The things you said at the beginning of your lecture (the introduction).
- The things you said at the end of your lecture (the summary).
- The way in which you presented the subject.

As mentioned previously, introduce the main issue you would like to convey and its major points. At the end of your lecture repeat what you said in the introduction—using the exact same words! During the bulk of your lecture, talk about all the rest. In most cases, however, the third point is the crucial one. What really matters is the way in which you present your lecture rather than its content. People tend to forget very quickly what they were told. In contrast, people will remember the person who stood in front of them. They will remember whether or not his presentation was impressive.

Try to reconstruct the way you feel and react when you run across a winning salesperson, an impressive lecturer, or an amazing teacher. You will no doubt remember that person the minute you see her again. Just by looking at her you know that you are in the presence of a formidable force. She delivers a message with confidence, and her impressive presence gets engraved in our memory.

It always surprises me to discover expert, knowledgeable, and experienced lecturers or salespeople who have at their disposal an incredible product but are unable to camouflage their shy personalities. Such people speak quietly and hardly look at the audience. They simply aren't aware of their poor performance and the message they convey. If you think you're such a person, think again. All it takes is practice, as the old saying goes: Fake it, until you make it.

At the end of this chapter, I'll teach you a special method using "mental gesture keys," which will remind you to perform unique gestures during your lecture. These gestures include raising your voice, smiling, staying silent for a few seconds, and telling a joke.

PRESENTATIONS 101: CHOOSING KEY IMAGES

The best way to remember what you want to say in a lecture, speech, lesson, sales presentation, or any other public speaking engagement is by using key words. More specifically, make use of the key images method.

We have learned how to memorize study material by using key images such as a hook or hanger. We may make use of these images to remind us of an idea, notion, phrase, or point about which we would like to talk. We may even use this method to remember a single, powerful sentence that is important for us to say using specific words. When we use key images, we're simply incapable of forgetting anything specific, since we aren't trying to remember anything specific. We're free to say anything we would like to without the pressure of needing to say exact words.

You're already familiar with the Roman room method. You've learned how to turn words or ideas into a specific image that's easy to imagine and remember. We've hung these words on different hooks in our mental files; the rooms in our homes are these files.

But first let's go back to the ancient Roman era. Let's prepare a short lecture—specifically, a sales presentation by a Roman salesman—according to the rules we have learned.

Billus Maximus Gatesus is the sales representative for Microsoftus, which manufactures a new, sophisticated product intended for use in gladiator arenas. This is a large exhibition window that controls the number of gladiators and lions entering the arenas and shuts down automatically when one of them attempts to escape. The name of this product is, of course, Windows MCXLLLV. Its main aim is to replace the large, heavy wooden gates that had been used up until now.

Billus Gatesus is about to participate in a bid that was announced by the Culture and Amusement Department of the City of Rome. Six companies offered their services for this bid. Gatesus's first step in preparing his sales pitch is determining the message he desires to bring across. He chooses his strongest sales pitches and turns them into single key images.

The message: "It's the end of the wooden gates—the future belongs to Windows."
Key image: a wooden gate

Sales point 1: Windows MCXLLLV opens horizontally. This allows for an effective, dramatic entrance into the ring. All the current arenas use heavy wooden gates that open vertically. This sophisticated window is new and dramatic, and it includes a red curtain that lifts up.
Key image: a red curtain

Sales point 2: simple activation. There's no need for ten muscular slaves to open the gates. It's easy for two men to operate Windows MCXLLLV. This makes for significant savings in the human resources budget.
Key image: ten strong slaves.

Sales point 3: Windows MCXLLLV is less expensive than wooden gates. The shelf price is 1,900 RD (Roman dollars). The discounted price offered to the

Culture and Amusement Department of the City of
Rome is 1,500 RD. At this price, the package includes
a huge, 26-by-32-foot window, a luxurious red satin
curtain with all the extra accessories, a ten-year warranty, and a special bonus—a two-ton, extra-grouchy
African lion!
Key image: two coins

Gatesus has completed writing down his main theme and
strong sales points. He is free to continue on to the other topics he'd like to elaborate on during the few minutes he has
left:

The Microsoftus company profile. This profile includes
the organization's structure, sales volume, equity
capital, and so on.
Key image: company logo

The company's product line.
Key image: a black line with six white spots
(representing six additional products)

Client list: Caligula Coliseum, Verona Congress Center,
Napoli YMCA, and Shea Stadium in Constantinople.
Key image: four customers

Let's go over the key images once more: the wooden gates
(it's the end of the wooden gates—the future belongs to Windows MCXLLLV), a red curtain (a horizontal opening versus a vertical opening), ten muscular slaves (no need for them
now), two coins (the shelf price verses the discounted price);
the company logo (Microsoftus company profile), a black
line with six white spots (the company's product line), and

four customers (the company's current customers and the products they use).

There are two options that may be used for the next step. The one we've already discussed involves opening a mental file, a predetermined room, and hanging these key images on its fixed hooks or pieces of furniture. The second method is more advanced, and that's what we'll explore next.

THE LECTURE HALL METHOD

There is only one thing better than our imagination, and that's reality.

The lecture hall method is actually the Roman room method, only this time, instead of linking key images or words to a familiar room we imagine in our home, we can hook the key images to a room right before our eyes—the actual venue in which our presentation will take place.

This method is applicable only if you're familiar with the venue. It may be a room in which you have taught before, your company's conference room, or maybe an auditorium which you have visited before. For example, if you know that your lecture will take place in your company's conference room, go inside that room and look around. Search for items on which you may hang your lecture's key images. Stand where you'll present your talk and scan the room, either clockwise or counterclockwise. As you stand there, take your key image list and hang the ideas on the items in the room.

Let's go back to our friend Billus Gatesus and place him in a time machine. Fast-forward a few centuries and imagine him in a modern company's conference room. What might he see around him? Perhaps a door, a flowerpot, a cabinet, a television, windows, paintings, and a bookshelf.

He may be able to connect the main theme of his lecture

to the door he sees in front of him—the wooden gate. Easy, right? Next to the door stands a large flowerpot. Using his imagination, he can put the flowerpot behind a red curtain. These two images will remind him of his first sales pitch.

He can then lift the cabinet near the flowerpot with the help of ten muscular slaves in an attempt to keep the cabinet from falling. After that, he could imagine two huge coins stuck to the sides of the television screen. The coins look like Mickey Mouse ears.

Using this method, you could hang every key image of your presentation to an item in the very room you're in. During the presentation, the only thing you need to do is look around. I promise you that the minute your eyes settle on a certain item in the room, the key image will pop into your head.

But what if the lecture is moved at the last minute and will be held in a different room? No problem here either. You already know how to use the traditional Roman room method. Since you're also obviously familiar with your company's conference room, it can be added temporarily to the rooms you have filed in your mind.

REVIEWING THE IMAGES

Let's return to our Roman friend and see how he did on his presentation. In Billus Gatesus's mind, the key images for his presentation are already attached to the items in the conference room (or any other room he has chosen). So he scans the conference room to make sure that the key images are vividly connected to the items.

He first looks to the conference room's cabinet, and the key image fails to pop into his head. His solution is to strengthen the associative bond. He decides that the image of the slaves holding the cabinet in the air needs to be changed. So now the slaves are bouncing the cabinet up and down in the air. He can see beads of sweat forming on their brows as they exert themselves. The associative bond is now strong and effective.

He reviews his presentation once more. This time, as he is touring the conference room in his imagination, he is talking to himself out loud. He does this again, but now he tracks the time it takes him to talk about each and every subject. He's speaking easily and smoothly in front of an imaginary audience. Spontaneous words flow forth without a trace of premeditated, rigid wording.

SHOWTIME

The morning of the presentation, Gatesus rehearses one last time. A minute prior to the presentation, our favorite Roman enters the conference room, butterflies fluttering about in the pit of his stomach. Board members of the Culture and Amusement Department of the City of Rome track his every move. Suddenly he sees, to his great anxiety, Caligula—the Caesar himself—sitting at the head of the table. He is even more surprised to see Caligula's horse sitting right next to him. He looks Caligula in the eye, and thinks: "Why should I get all worked up about this? The guy brought his horse to my sales presentation. What could be worse than this?" Now he feels ready and willing to wow them with his sales presentation.

As he stands at the front of the room, Billus Gatesus starts his mental tour of the conference room. He looks at the door and immediately remembers the wooden gate, his first key image. With great confidence and authority he begins his lecture: "Your Majesty, revered citizens of Rome, distinguished horse—I'm here to make an announcement to you. Wooden gates are dead—the future belongs to Windows MCXLLLV!"

He pauses momentarily and looks at his audience; they are

impressed. He looks at the flowerpot next to the door. He is happily surprised to see that the red curtain has been lifted, revealing the flowerpot. He emphasizes the dramatic effect that will take place as the gladiators and lions enter the arena after a red curtain is horizontally raised. His audience is even more impressed.

He moves on to the cabinet. Now he sees the slaves bouncing it in the air. He surprises his audience: "The need for ten muscular and expensive slaves is a thing of the past." The board members gasp in shock.

Moving on to the TV screen, he imagines two Mickey Mouse ears. These are the two large coins. Gatesus continues: "And all this for just 1,900 Roman dollars. Yet since Microsoftus views you as an important customer, we would like to offer you a special package deal for 1,500 RD, which includes the following: a huge, 26-by-32-foot window, a luxurious red satin curtain with all the extra accessories, a ten-year warranty, and a special bonus—a two-ton African lion! This beast is gladiator-proof, and after being put on a starvation plan, it's extra grouchy." He pauses yet again.

The board members are amazed. Caligula's horse loses consciousness over the story of the lion. And our man continues on his path to glory. At the end of his speech, he receives a standing ovation. On the spot, Caligula orders twenty Windows MCXLLLV package deals for all the arenas in Rome.

Mission accomplished.

THE GESTURE KEYS

There isn't a big difference between a stage actor and a lecturer. They both perform in front of an audience. Both of them need to make the audience understand who they are and what their character is. And the two do so by acting.

They need to remember at what exact moment it's necessary to raise their voice, smile, pause, move, and cross their arms. The stage actor uses exaggerated behaviors such as extreme tones of voice, hand gestures, wild laughter, hot tears—whatever it takes to capture his audience. The lecturer is an actor as well. If he isn't one, he may very likely be achingly boring.

The lecturer, however, must refrain from acting in an exaggerated way. When a lecture seems too dramatic, it will be perceived as fake and the lecturer will come across as untrustworthy.

Mark Twain once said that a ten-minute spontaneous lecture required of him at least three hours of preparation. Any change in the tone of speech, every gesture, and every movement were meticulously planned. As we've said, there's no need for a meticulous plan, just as there's no need to lock in certain words or gestures. But those of us who aren't natural actors can certainly use the help of additional hooks.

Let's say you wish to raise your voice to camouflage an exceptionally weak argument. Take the case in which you think it's necessary to pause briefly after a meaningful sentence (the kind that needs to be "digested"). Think of when you would like to nod in approval, tell a joke, or sum up an idea with a question. In order to remember to make such verbal and physical gestures, it's possible to add "key gestures" to our key images.

Say Gatesus plans to sum up the sales pitch involving the ten slaves with a question mark. He might ask: "Only two people are required to operate these windows—simply amazing, isn't it?" In order to remember this, he can create an additional key, an additional image. He could imagine a giant question mark and tie it to the item to which he has already connected the slaves. On the top of the cabinet (made of dark mahogany) are engraved black question marks. These question marks aren't meant to be on such elegant furniture. When he reaches this image during his presentation, he will envision the slaves bouncing the cabinet. Yet, along with this image, he will see the question marks engraved on it. All this will remind him that he wishes to stress his point.

You can create a variety of keys, or images, that describe a specific gesture:

> A *loudspeaker* will remind you of the need to raise your voice.
>
> A *light bulb* will remind you to look particularly expressive when you make a certain point.
>
> A giant *stop sign* will remind you to pause for four seconds after a specific pitch.
>
> A yellow *smiley button* will remind you to smile or tell a joke related to the subject.

You can easily add the gesture keys to the key images. As you prepare your lecture, write down as many key images and gestures as you desire.

You might hesitate at the idea of remembering a large amount of key words, fearing that your brain won't be able to manage all of them. But don't worry. At the end of your lecture, you'll be surprised at how easy it was to remember all the connections. And that's not all—your brain would have been very capable of remembering even more key images.

〜〜〜〜〜〜〜〜

CHAPTER 17

"ME TALK . . .
YOU UNDERSTAND . . ."

A Super Memory
for Languages and Vocabulary

Two guys are eating noodles for lunch.
"Explain to me," the first says. "Why are these
things that we're eating called noodles?"
"What do you mean?" the second responds as
he pushes another forkful into his mouth.
"They're long like noodles, they're soft like
noodles, and they taste like noodles. Why
shouldn't we call them noodles?"

WHILE THE FIRST noodle may have originated in China,
the word comes from the German-Yiddish *nudel* or *nutel*.
There are countless other examples of words that English
has adopted from other languages. Here are a few others:
ballet (French), *bureau* (French), *ketchup* (Malay), *yogurt*

(Turkish), *taboo* (Tongan), *karma* (Sanskrit), and *whatsamad-dahwityou* (Brooklynese).

Some words are named after people: *chauvinist* in its original sense of "blind or exaggerated patriotism" comes from the (perhaps legendary) Nicolas Chauvin, a soldier in Napoleon's army, who was completely and utterly devoted to the emperor long after Napoleon was deposed. *Nicotine* is derived from the name of Jean Nicot, French ambassador to Portugal in the 1500s, who introduced tobacco to the French court. The *sandwich* is named after John Montagu, the fourth Earl of Sandwich, an obsessive gambler who asked his servant to serve him his meals on bread, allowing him to gamble without pausing to wield a knife and fork. Leopold von Sacher-Masoch, an Austrian writer, who found pleasure in self-induced physical torture, gave his name to the word *masochism*.

A foreign language often seems to be a heaping tangle of illogical pronunciations and pauses. When we hear a conversation in Chinese between two people, we may wonder how they can possibly understand each other. There's no doubt that the best way to learn a language is to travel to the country where that language is spoken and stay there awhile. Constant exposure to native speakers will get you speaking and understanding any foreign tongue before long.

It is, however, also possible to learn a foreign language using the trusty memory methods you're about to encounter.

ALL ABOUT COMPLIANT PEOPLE AND STUBBORN PEOPLE

I know a few people who describe themselves as lacking any talent for grasping a new language. Yet this type of person, if sent into exile in a different country, will come to speak the local language fluently within a few years. So there's no question here of one sort of talent or another. It's all a matter of willingness.

A very rich and famous American-born businessman living in Israel once invited me for a private memory lesson.

"I've been living in Israel for thirty years and I can't speak Hebrew. Please teach me memory techniques that will enable me to memorize the language," he pleaded, as we sat in his living room of luxury.

"I'm sorry," I apologized. "But I can't help you. You can't learn Hebrew."

He shifted uncomfortably in his armchair.

"And why do you say that?" he retorted.

"Because you have the same problem as Tony Bennett," I replied. "You left your heart in San Francisco. You never tried to assimilate. You never thought it important enough to learn Hebrew. Why bother if everyone in Israel knows English, right?"

A different problem also lies in our willingness to forgive ourselves for misspellings, diction errors, and other mistakes. Such mistakes get assimilated into our private lexicon and become habit. My father, for instance, who was of Czech origin, never learned how to pronounce "Wednesday" properly, since "Wednesday" isn't pronounced the same way it is spelled. If it was pronounced as it's written, we would say "Wed-nes-day." But in actuality we pronounce it as "Wensday," disregarding the first *d* and second *e*. (By the way, the word is borrowed from Old English *Wodnes daeg*. That was the day dedicated to the god Wodnes.) My father didn't consider his blunder important enough to fix. But at least he was willing to make mistakes.

Some people fail to acquire a language because they

pressure themselves to be perfect. They're afraid to make a mistake and "lose face," so they prefer to remain silent. I see that especially in the Far East. When I give seminars in Japan, Korea, and China, the participants hardly say a word. They do learn English, but they are too embarrassed that their English is not good enough to use at all.

So here's a directive for those of you who are too timid to give the language you're learning a whirl: talk . . . and make mistakes! It's the only way to learn. Language is a living practice. You must talk and accept the fact that you will not lose face if you make mistakes.

Several years ago my wife and I went to Paris. My wife speaks French (you know, Strasbourg), and one day we went to a metro stop and my wife approached the ticket seller.

"Je voudrais acheter deux billets pour le metro, s'il vous plaît," she requested in perfect French, asking to buy two tickets for the metro.

The next day, before taking the metro again, I said to her: "Today, my dear, I'll buy the tickets."

"No way!" she shouted. "Your French is terrible."

"It's really important to practice the language. Let me show you how easy it is," I replied.

With a strut of confidence, I approached the clerk, smiled, raised two fingers, and said: "Deux!"

What can I tell you? I was given the two same tickets she'd gotten for us the previous day.

It takes between six hundred and one thousand words to get by in a language. That's all! Six hundred to one thousand of the most commonly used words will enable you to understand 75.6 percent of any foreign newspaper, according to several studies in linguistics. (Even better news: it takes only thirty words to be able to read the sports section.) So if you learn twenty words a day, in just one month you can read a daily newspaper and understand the underlying ideas in any language you choose! Isn't that encouraging?

The real question, however, is how someone can learn twenty words a day in a systematic way that will permanently etch those words into memory.

For starters, be sure you understand the word.

Take note of the following sentences: "Today's youth are so decadent"; "Mom says Aunt Sue makes the best apple strudel ever"; "That vase is so amorphous." You must have come across the words *decadent*, *strudel*, and *amorphous* before. But let's be honest: do you know what they really mean?

The message I'm trying to convey (and I've said this before) is that many words remain meaningless to us even when they're from our mother tongue. Usually this is the result of the embarrassment we think we would face if we were to admit that we don't know what the expression means. Someone tells us that the Eastern European market is in a state of stagnation. We nod knowingly, but we're clueless. And we'll never admit to the fact that we have no idea what this really means. Our ego will not allow us to ask, lest we be considered a total idiot.

Art Linkletter once had a TV show that featured a segment in which he talked to young children. On one show, he asked the children: "Do you know anyone who has charisma?" The kids, who had no idea what the word meant but were aware they were on TV, began improvising answers.

"I think my uncle has charisma," one of them said. "He's been in the hospital for two weeks now."

"My mom's friend had charisma," a cute girl replied. "But she was able to get rid of it. I just can't remember what shampoo she used."

"My neighbor has several charismas," a third boy bragged. "But they haven't bloomed yet."

When cute kids say the darnedest things, we find it quite amusing. But when *we* try the same trick, all our good intentions simply go down the drain. So if you wish to remember words in order to use them, first make sure that you understand their meaning.

As mentioned, make a new habit for yourself. Learn new words every single day. After you've learned a word, use it as often as possible. Make up sentences and try to weave the new word into them. Use these words while conversing with a friend. The more you use new words, the faster they will become an integral part of your communication.

THE HISTORY OF A WORD

Every language has words that are unique to the local culture, and some are simply untranslatable. These words are irrelevant to other cultures, or there was simply no need to translate them. For example, in an Eskimo language (or so I've heard), there are seven words that describe different types of snow. Presumably only the Eskimos know the difference between the types of the cold, white stuff. On the other hand, there's no translation for the word *sand* in that language.

We may also sometimes encounter a word that initially seems unrelated to anything we know, but if we dig further, it could very well be a word we can relate to. Take the word *acrophobia*. *Phobia*, as we know, means "fear" (think *claustrophobia*, fear of being in enclosed places). Let's take the prefix *acro-* and see if there's another word we're familiar with that contains it. How about *acrobat*? An acrobat is a skilled gymnastic performer, many of whom walk on a tightrope way up high and perform daring flips. Such people are called acrobats since *acro-* means "high." Acrophobia, then, is the fear of heights! Try to find the roots of the words you'd like to understand, and from where they're derived.

The English language is a potpourri of Latin, Greek, French, German, Italian, and numerous other languages. Understanding its origins helps with the study of European foreign languages, as you can often find a similar or parallel word to English. In French, *livre* means "book." Is there a word in English that sounds like *livre*? Yes, there is—*library*!

And what about the German word *vater*? That's "father." What's the German word for light? *Licht*. What does the word *haus* mean? Easy, isn't it? "House," just as in English.

Many words have the same prefix or suffix in English and in other languages—for example, a trans-Siberian train or a transatlantic flight. The Latin prefix *trans-* means "crossing." Knowing that the Greek prefix *dis-* means "lack of" or "not" makes it easier to understand the meaning of words such as *disability* or *disoriented*. Crack open a dictionary or head to an online dictionary site, and you've got a terrific memory tool at your fingertips.

HOW TO LEARN FOREIGN LANGUAGES QUICKLY . . . AND FOR LIFE

You will not always be able to determine the meaning of a foreign word using a similar word in a different language. But once you know what a word means you should be able to remember it using other methods you've learned. All you need to do is find an association to that foreign word. You could find an alternative word, or words that sound similar to it.

Let's go back to *acrophobia*. Take this word and once again separate it into two parts: *acro* and *phobia*. *Phobia*, as we said, means "fear." Now we have to take the prefix *acro-* and turn it into a meaningful word or image. We'll start by taking the meaning of the full word *acrophobia*, "fear of heights," and connect it to a new image we'll create.

For example, imagine that you're in ancient Greece, standing at the site of the ruins of the Acropolis in Athens. You are up high, looking down on the destruction, when the fear of heights attacks you. The image you've now created is that of a person standing at the top of the Acropolis suffering from a fear of heights, which brings a whole new meaning to the word *acrophobia*.

What does *vertigo* really mean? In English, it's a sensation of dizziness. How can we remember the meaning of this word? Let's imagine a man standing in the middle of the street, spinning around and asking: "Vertigo? Ver-ti-go? Where to go?"

Suppression means forceful prevention of someone to act as he wills. Let's divide the word into two sound-alike words *super-* and *pressure*. The image we could create is that of "strong pressure." And what is suppression if not a strong pressure applied to a person, group, or nation against their will?

Traveling to several places simultaneously is impossible. But it's certainly possible to learn and speak several languages at the same time. Some people can speak three, four, even ten languages; some can speak a lot more.

A man stands in front of the check-in counter at the airport and says to the airline representative: "I would like this black suitcase to fly to Paris, the red one to London, the brown bag to Rome, the green backpack to Prague, and I myself would like to fly to New York."

Astonished, the representative stares at him and says: "Sir, I'm sorry, but there's no way we can do such a thing."

"But why?" the man replies. "Last time I used your airline that's exactly what you did."

The Italian cardinal Giuseppe Caspar Mezzofanti (1774–1849) was a well-known linguist and hyperpolyglot who spoke thirty-eight languages and about thirty dialects. Emil Krebs (1867–1930) was a German traveler and expert on China who mastered sixty-eight languages, among them Mongolian, Javanese, Manchurian, and Ainu. He also spoke four dialects of Spanish—Guipuzcoa, Bizcaya, Laburdi, and Zuberoan. I too speak Zuberoan, a dialect in the Basque region of northern Spain, but for some reason when I'm there, the people always ignore me when I say something.

Let's learn Spanish—the "regular" kind. The meaning of the word *queso* in English is "cheese." What word in English sounds like the word *queso*? *Case!* All you have to do is imagine that in Spain, or in any other Spanish-speaking country, cheese is sold only in leather cases. There's a Brie case, a Parmesan case, a bleu cheese case, and so on. Anytime you need to remember how to say "cheese" in Spanish, remember that cheese is a case. The word *case* will remind you of the word *queso*.

How do you say "milk" in Spanish? *Leche*. The word *leche* is reminiscent of the word *lychee*, the Chinese fruit. Imagine that milk cartons contain lychee milk as well as cow's milk.

The Spanish word *playa* means "beach," and what does that sound like? In my opinion, *player*. Think how the beach is a gathering place for football players in Spain. Imagine thousands of players crowding the beach, which makes it impossible to find a spot where you can spread out your beach towel.

Now let's learn some French. French is a language that—in order to sound its best—requires painful-sounding moans and groans. Do you know what the French word for "egg" is? I know the word is spelled *oeuf*. But how's it pronounced? Something between "eff" and "oof," and no matter how you say it, the French will be offended.

Don't give up hope. There is a way to tackle this language. In French, the word for "war" is *guerre* (sounds like "ger"). Imagine that in all of France's wars, its soldiers wore gray trench coats. Gray trench coats: Gray = "ger" = *guerre* = war. Another association could be Richard Gere. If so, imagine Richard Gere returning from the battlefield.

Here are a few more examples. *Chien* is "dog," so imagine a dog with a chain. The French word for "tree" is *arbre*, similar to our *harbor*, so let's imagine a harbor in which only trees are docking—no boats or ships, only trees.

Time for a little test. See what you remember from what we have just learned:

Leche _____
Queso _____
Suppression _____
Vertigo _____
What is the word for "fear of heights"? _____
What is "war" in French? _____
What is "dog" in French? _____

And of course, most important of all, give life to these words and use them as often as possible.

YIDDIBRISH: THE JEWISH MULTILINGUAL SYSTEM

For those learning a foreign language, the hope is that thousands of new words will be remembered just when they're needed in conversation. But what happens when someone wants to communicate and doesn't exactly know how? This is what happened with the Jews until Hebrew became a modern language in the nineteenth century.

The problem was that Hebrew was a holy language used only in prayer and sacred books. It didn't fulfill the basic function of a language, namely, to serve as a means of communication between individuals. In order to conduct business, exchange ideas, or just buy groceries, Jews around the world used the local language, be it Arabic, Persian, German, or French. Over time, from generation to generation, not everyone was so strict about going to synagogue or learning, yet Hebrew survived! Thousands of years after it had been created, thousands of years after it was last spoken aloud, the language persevered. Today it's a thriving language and the mother tongue of Israelis, going back a few generations already.

Think about it for a moment. A language that *wasn't* spoken at all was preserved in its entirety! And how was it, exactly, that the Jews were able to maintain the language? By using an unusual strategy. In each community, they invented a new language that was a combination of biblical Hebrew and whatever the local language may have been. By always incorporating Hebrew into their speech, they safeguarded the language of the Jewish people.

The two most famous languages Jews created are Ladino and Yiddish. Ladino, or Spanyolit, is primarily Castilian Spanish, with Hebrew mixed in. In 1492, Jews who refused to renounce their religion and convert to Catholicism were kicked out of Spain by King Ferdinand and Queen Isabella. It's estimated that between 100,000 and 200,000 Jews were forced to leave Spain during that time. These Jews continued to speak Ladino in their new homes, such as London, Amsterdam, Hamburg, Italy, Constantinople, and Thessalonica.

When Ladino was at its peak as a spoken language, an extensive body of literature was written using it, including Torah expositions, dramas, and biographies. Gradually, additional words from Turkish, Greek, and many other local languages spoken by the Spanish Jews (known now as Sephardic Jews) made their way into the language. *Cada uno es sadik en sus ojos* in Ladino means "Every man is a tzaddik in his own right." They retained the Hebrew word *tzaddik* (righteous person), for example.

Yiddish served the same purpose for Ashkenazi Jews (European Jews) that Ladino served for Sephardic Jews. The only difference is that Yiddish, which is Hebrew mixed with German, was a much more popular language spoken by many more people in a different part of the world.

Once, most Ashkenazi Jews spoke Yiddish. Most scholars believe that Yiddish was already spoken in the eleventh century by Jews who left northern France to settle in the Rhine Valley. The language spread, and soon, whether a Jew found himself in Russia, Germany, New York, or Buenos Aires, he could communicate with other Jews. The word *Yiddish*, by the way, comes from *yid* or *jid*, meaning "Jew," and *dish*, meaning *Deutsch*, "German." In other words, Jewish German.

Hebrew words found in Jewish holy books also entered the popular, secular Yiddish language. Take the phrase *mama lashon*, "mother tongue," as an example. *Mama* is German for "mother," and *lashon* is "tongue" in Hebrew. Here's another example: *Bist ah batuach, uber shik eran mezumanim*— "I trust you, but send cash." *Batuach* is Hebrew for "trust" and *mezumanim* in the same language means "cash."

Yiddish as a whole is composed of about 15–20 percent Hebrew, 70 percent German, and 10 percent other languages such as Hungarian and Romanian. In addition, and most interestingly, Yiddish is written with Hebrew letters in order to preserve the Hebrew writing system. Yiddish helped Jews all over the world stay connected to Hebrew and, in turn, keep that language alive and active.

INFUSE NEW, FOREIGN WORDS INTO YOUR CONVERSATIONS

Let's take the word *dinero*—"money" in Spanish. Think of several ways in which you're likely to talk about money, but substitute the word *dinero* for the word money: "How much *dinero* do you have? I need to borrow $50." "The only thing that you care about is *dinero, dinero, dinero.*" "He's a rich man. He's got a lot of *dinero* in the bank."

Here's another Spanish word—*hombre.* It means "man." "What a nice *hombre.* He helped me fix my car." "See that *hombre* there . . . the one with the red hat? I can tell that that *hombre* has a lot of *dinero.*"

Let's add *quiero*—"I want." "*Quiero* peace in the world." "*Quiero* much health for my family." "*Quiero* a good cake. That's what I really *quiero* right now." "*Quiero* to be a *hombre* with a lot of *dinero.*"

This technique is good for someone who wants to become functional in a language. Someone who wants to learn how to speak a language correctly and fluently needs to study the language's fundamentals, including how to conjugate its verbs and decline its nouns. This is merely a fun way to get started. As you acquire more and more words using this method, it becomes easier to learn a language's other components because you've already developed a certain level of confidence and understanding.

WRITING WITHOUT "MISSPELLATIONS"

Another bothersome problem people have is spelling words correctly.

Yes, I'm aware we have spell-checkers to do the job for us. So what's next? Talkers that will talk for us? Walkers that will travel for us? How lazy *is* mankind? Find out once and for all how to spell a word correctly.

In order to remember how to spell a word correctly, isolate the problem. This means checking to see which letters in a word are the source of the problem.

For example, take the word *friend*. To remember how to spell this word, you need to remember the "*i* before *e* except after *c*" rule.

What about the word *conceal*? Here the problem lies within the *ea* combination. Let's make up a sentence that incorporates the meaning of the word—for instance, "The elephant conceals the ant." Using the same order of words in the sentence, the *e* of *elephant* comes first, and the *a* of *ant* appears afterward. Besides, logic says that the ant isn't capable of concealing an elephant, right? The elephant is larger, so it's in front. So "The elephant conceals the ant" is clear: the *e* precedes the *a*.

What about other words that don't have cute reminders to go along with them? Look at the word *necessary*. Let's isolate the problem, which is, in essence, the question of how many times a *c* or an *s* should appear in the word, and where exactly they should be placed. The word *cat* will represent the letter *c*, while the word *sunset* represent the two *s*'s. Now our sentence will be "It's necessary for the cat to watch the sunset." What do you think? Two for the price of one! Now we know that the *c* appears first, and that there are two *s*'s.

You can also try isolating the letters you always write incorrectly. In the word *occasionally*, we have two *c*'s that come first and then a single *s*. Let's turn this idea into a sentence: "Occasionally, I drink 100 cc of soda a day." This is how we can remember what letter precedes the others.

Another great system you can use is reverse acronyms.

Want to remember how to spell *rythem*, or *rithem* . . . uh, I mean, *rhythm*? Try "Rhythm helps your two hips move." What about *arithmetic*? "A rat in the house may eat the ice cream." Reverse acronyms can help you remember how to spell a word too. Begin by turning the word *acronym* into a backronym. Go for it!

> *acronym*: A-_____ C-_____ R-_____ O-_____
> N-_____ Y-_____ M-_____

And finally, let me introduce you to the following word:

aequeosalinocalcalinoceraceoaluminosocupreovitriolic

This is one of the longest English words, and it describes the water composition in the springs of Bristol, England.

Happily, odds are that you'll never need to memorize it or come up with an acronym to remember how to spell it. But you could really rack up some points in Scrabble if you use it . . .

~~~~~~~~~~~~~~~~~~~~~~~

CHAPTER 18

"HELLO, RON— I MEAN DON . . . UH, JOHN"

IN ONE OF my favorite cafés, I noticed a waiter giving special attention to a customer: "How's everything, Lizzie? . . . Are you happy with your dish, Lizzie? . . . Lizzie, would you like more salad dressing?"

After Lizzie had paid and left, I had a short conversation with the waiter.

"Well done," I complimented him. "Such a customer, whose name you remembered and whom you doted on with such personal and devoted service, will no doubt be loyal and spread the word about your excellent service."

"Thanks very much, that's very kind of you." The waiter smiled with satisfaction. "But that was my wife."

. . .

Okay, so that was easy. But think of King Solomon. He had a thousand wives to remember.

> King Solomon: Hi, Sarah.
> Hannah: I'm Hannah.
> King Solomon: You're not my wife?
> Hannah: Not yet.

A person's name is his or her most prized possession. In one way or another, we all want our name to be associated with greatness of some kind. A prominent name could lead us to immortality, or so we hope. Our name reflects who we are and what we leave behind, for good and for bad. God said to King David, "I have made thee a great name, like unto the name of the great men that are in the earth." To Abraham He said, "And I will make of thee a great nation, and I will bless thee, and make thy name great; and thou shalt be a blessing."

It's because of this that we should approach a person's name with the highest respect. Most of us falter in this. We meet someone, and within minutes of parting, we don't remember the person's name. We think, "Wait a second. What was that guy's name?" We weren't paying attention!

A person's name is usually given by their parents. That doesn't necessarily mean that the person would have given himself that specific name. Maybe that's why we don't pay such close attention to names. In other words, if people were to choose their own names, we really would pay more attention. We would find them interesting because we would see the meaning that the individuals had attached to them. It'd be interesting to learn if Grace's parents, for example, were correct in giving her that name. Is Grace indeed gracious and compassionate? Has Harry grown up to be brave and strong?

Has Pearl turned into a woman with internal beauty and a gentle spirit?

King David was commanded to call his son Solomon (Shlomo, which means "peaceful" in Hebrew): "For his name shall be Solomon, and I will give peace and quietness unto Israel in his days." Like King David, many parents sometimes feel that divine inspiration rests behind the names they select for their children.

But since we know that a person's name is more of an issue of chance (or that a person was named after a relative who has no real meaning to us), we have no special inspiration to remember names.

That's why prior to an encounter, you must keep this in mind: you are going to meet new people, and you must attempt to remember their names.

When we arrive at a new event, most of us exchange names for the sake of formality and not because the people we meet truly interest us. In fact, we concentrate on ourselves instead of other people.

Prior to an event where we are likely to meet new people, be it a convention, trade show, or social gathering, we must concentrate and focus on remembering the names of people we meet. When you see the entrance to the reception hall or the young hostess welcoming you, develop the habit of reiterating silently, "I am about to enter an event where I'll meet new, interesting, and unique people. I must pay attention to their names and try to remember them."

HOW TO REMEMBER PEOPLE AT A NEW EVENT

First, behave nicely. Don't hit or annoy new people, unless you desperately need attention or someone has parked in your reserved parking space.

When you meet someone new and exchange names, be sure that you heard and understood the person's name. If you did not, ask him or her to repeat it. Embarrassing? On the contrary! Your request shows that you have a genuine interest in the person.

If you see an old, familiar face and you happen to remember the person's name, it's advisable to make the first move by introducing yourself and avoiding the other person's embarrassment should he not remember your name. Don't test others' memories.

"Hi, Michael," you say as you shake hands. "I'm Fred. We met at Simon and Garfunkel's party last year. I was the one who spilled wine on your wife's white dress." (Well, I guess Michael would have remembered you in this case.)

This type of approach changes worlds. Michael will be grateful that you didn't test him and will appreciate the fact that you remembered his name. This is a win-win approach— you've earned endearment and admiration, and possibly have made a new friend. (Only after you've offered to reimburse him for the dry cleaning bill, of course.)

When meeting a new acquaintance, study the business card you've been handed for the correct way to spell the person's name. Commiserate with Craig or Ellen about how annoying it can be when someone says Greg instead of Craig, or Helen instead of Ellen. Stressing the correct pronunciation is flattering and generates gratitude that the person's name really matters to you.

Repeat the name verbally immediately after you read or hear it for the first time. "Pleased to meet you, Bill Gates. My name is Donald Fitzgerald Duck. Where do you work, Bill? Ah, I see that you are the chairperson of a software company. Interesting. I haven't heard about you, but I'm sure you've heard about me—Donald's Pest Control? We've got branches all over the United States. Where are you located, Bill? Seattle? We've got a branch not far from you in San Diego."

Repeat the name often during the conversation while mentioning details associated with the person, such as where you met and his profession. This is a method of engraving a network of associative links in your memory.

"So, Bill, how are you enjoying London? Yes, I couldn't find a normal coffee shop open after eight at night there either, but I did locate a Starbucks in Leicester Square, Bill, and another one in Scotland. Back home in Glen Heights, the coffee shop is open until midnight, although by eleven there's no coffee left."

Take a genuine interest in the person. Ask leading questions and look for common topics of interest. We remember people whom we find interesting. Perhaps the woman opposite you also collects seahorses or peach pits.

"By the way, Sophia, I saw that you ate a peach earlier on. Did you by chance save the pit? I have an amazing collection of pits in my living room." Surely you agree that this is an excellent teaser for an introductory conversation. Or perhaps not . . .

IT'S GREEK TO ME

"Their names all sound the same and are impossible to pronounce—Xiou, Hsing, or Xue," some Westerners tend to complain about Asian names.

A Japanese diplomat once expressed to me a similar sentiment: his difficulty in differentiating between "all those Western names," which all sounded the same to him. "How can you tell the difference between Larry, Harry, Henry, Harvey, and Harold?" he asked me in desperation.

One way is to ask Mr. Wong or Mrs. Yoshimoto to explain the meaning of their names. The name Baker lacks meaning for the Chinese, just as Wong or Wei lacks meaning for Westerners. However, if we understand that the meaning of Wei is "strong" and Wong is "orchid," it would be easier for us to differentiate between and memorize the names. Suddenly the name has meaning—something that we can imagine.

The Indian name Deepak (as in the spiritual teacher Deepak Chopra) means "light." Wolfgang, a German name, is not a pack of wolves but "the path of the wolf." Alexander, a common Greek name, means "protector of mankind"—how's that for drama? Here are the meanings of some common Russian names: Lev (think Lev Tolstoy) means "lion"; Arkady is derived from the Greek *arctos,* meaning "bear"; Vladimir means "great ruler"; and the meaning of Natasha is "Christ's birthday."

My advice to those of you who conduct business with Chinese, Indian, Russian, or Icelandic counterparts is to spend a few minutes reading about the history, origins, and different meanings of their names. In addition to helping you remember their names, learning their meaning will also make for a good impression. There isn't a person who would not be awed by the fact that you took the trouble to check the origin and connotation of his or her name.

The next step is to convert the combination of sounds that create the name into something meaningful to remember. As mentioned previously, one of the best ways to accomplish this is by creating "sound-alike" associations.

For example:

- The name Bill could remind us of Bill Clinton, Buffalo Bill, or a dollar bill.

- Hiroshi could remind us of Hiroshima or the English word *hero*.
- Philip could be reminiscent of Prince Philip or the Philips Company.

Surnames are no exception:

- Bloomberg could conjure up the image of a hill blooming with flowers.
- Federman could be a "feather man" or someone using FedEx.
- Olivia Martinez might be a woman with a liking for a martini with an olive.

Having amused ourselves a little, let's get down to business and apply what we have learned.

CHAPTER 19

THE TOP METHODS FOR REMEMBERING PEOPLE

IN THE SIXTIES, two methods for compiling sketches of criminal suspects—Photo-FIT and Identi-Kit—were developed. They were based on eyewitnesses' abilities to reconstruct facial features from memory. Jacques Penry, who invented the Photo-FIT, claimed, "A person's face is the sum total of the parts and details of his face." Over time, the efficiency of these kits was found to be limited, since people do not really remember precise facial details. Research has shown that if an eyewitness is asked to reconstruct the face of the person sitting opposite him, he'll be just 18 percent accurate.

However, human memory is able to reconstruct four facial features quite accurately: the shape of the face (oval or round), hair (length, color), age, and anomalies (i.e., outstanding features such as a crooked nose, a glass eye, or gold teeth).

Now that you've met a few people at a reception, how are you going to etch them into your noggin?

The most well-known and popular technique for remembering names is based on creating associative links between a person's name and their appearance. Ahaziah, King of Israel, recognized the prophet Elijah as "a man with a garment of hair and with a leather belt around his waist," as recounted in Kings, and in the Song of Songs, King Solomon waxed poetic:

> *How beautiful you are, my darling!*
> *Oh, how beautiful!*
> *Your eyes behind your veil are doves.*
> *Your hair is like a flock of goats*
> *descending from Mount Gilead.*

Find a connection between someone's name and their appearance or personality. If, for example, you meet Richard, who's wearing an expensive Armani suit and Rolex watch, you can easily think of him as *Richard* the *Rich*.

Brad is a big, fat man. Imagine *Brad* eating a lot of *bread*— and don't those carbs just add up!

Beth wears clothes smeared with food and grime from her adoring children. Undoubtedly, *Beth* needs a *bath*.

You meet Dr. Jim Green at the anesthesiologists' annual awakening convention. Dr. Green is tall and muscular, and exudes machismo. We can play with sound-alikes and change his name from *Jim* to *Jeep* as we imagine him driving a green jeep over someone's meticulously manicured green lawn.

If Melody has a pleasant voice, imagine that she's a singer. Ah, lovely *Melody* sings *melodies* all the time.

Rose is tall with short hair. How can we remember her? How about imagining her with a wreath of *roses* on her head? This would help warm her head, which she'd surely appreciate because she has short hair.

For *Bernard Benedict,* imagine a *St. Bernard* dog with a barrel of *Benedictine* liqueur hanging from his neck.

Bill Gardener? Imagine a *gardener* working in the garden with former president Bill Clinton.

Use sound-alikes for Jose-Leon Margal. *Jose* is like *hose. Leon* is like *lion. Margal* sounds like *marble.* He used a hose to train a lion to balance on a marble. Why not?

Meet Julie Ferrero.

Julie is a retired VP of a very successful fashion company. She obviously accumulated *mucho dinero* and now enjoys spending it on *jewelry.* Jewelry will remind us of her name, Julie. Can you guess what brand of car she recently bought? I'm sure you immediately thought of a Ferrari. The *jewelry* and the *Ferrari* will assist us in remembering her name—Julie Ferrero.

Meet Wolfgang Achsman.

Wolfgang is a staff writer for *Der Frankfurter Allgemeine Zeitung.* His most prominent feature, the one that grabs our attention, is his million-dollar smile with its perfectly white teeth. (Don't you just hate these guys?) Sometimes journalists can be like a gang of wolves hunting down celebrities. Imagine Wolfgang leading the pack of wolves, devouring celebrities with his teeth and sharp pen. He hacks up celebrities' egos with his ruthless writing—they are cut down by his brutal "axe-man" powers. That's Wolfgang Achsman.

Each person has his own system of associations. What works for one person won't necessarily work for another. Someone may better remember the name Julie because he has a family member by the same name. Someone else might think of the actress Julie Andrews or the French novelist Jules Verne. The idea is to use the first association that jumps into your mind—that's usually the most effective one.

THE NICKNAME METHOD

Just slip out the back, Jack
Make a new plan, Stan
Don't need to be coy, Roy
Just get yourself free

PAUL SIMON, "50 Ways to Leave Your Lover"

Nicknames are another great way to remember names. (The word *nickname* actually comes from the fifteenth-century English word *ekename*, meaning "an additional name.") You can create a nickname, one that will describe the person, and add it to the person's name. This was done during Talmudic times with names such as Hillel the Old, Zeira the Young, Abba the Long, and Samuel the Small.

Throughout the ages, it's been common practice to use nicknames, often to distinguish between people with the same name—Little John, Long John Silver, Buffalo Bill, Ivan the Terrible, Red Daniel, Oscar the Grouch, Charles the Great, Charles the Beautiful, Charles the Mad, Babe Ruth, and Charles the Okay.

Former U.S. president George W. Bush is an avid fan of this method. He's widely known for assigning nicknames to journalists and politicians as a memory tool. His secretary of state,

Condoleezza Rice, was "Condi"; he called Russian president Vladimir Putin "Pootie-Poot"; "Danny boy" was his presidential counselor, Dan Bartlett; U.S. senator and former presidential candidate John McCain was "Hogan"; and his secretary of education was Margaret "La Margarita" Spellings.

The best sound-alike nicknames are those you can visualize.

Meet Kim Baker.

Kim is a guitar teacher. Look at her . . . doesn't she look kind? That's because she is kind Kim. She's so kind that she bakes cupcakes for her students. That's kind Kim Baker.

THE JFK METHOD

John Fitzgerald Kennedy didn't invent this method, but everyone knows who JFK is because of it. The basic idea is to use a person's initials in order to remember their name.

A former Navy SEAL officer named Jacob attended one of my seminars and taught the crowd a nice method for remembering names based on reverse acronyms (what I call "backronyms"). He was successful in recalling people's names by turning them into acronyms that described the person's personality. In the Navy, for example, he served with a guy named Jack. Jacob described **Jack** as being a nice guy who was a little hyperactive at times and prone to do stupid things. So Jacob turned his name into **J**ovial and **C**razy **K**id. That's how Jacob remembered his name.

Another guy, **Brian**, was an idiot who always broke the rules and even had a few run-ins with the law. So the appropriate acronym for his name became **B**reaks **R**ules **I**ntentionally **A**lways **N**aughty.

Then there was another soldier, **Tim**, who was Brian's polar opposite. Tim was a nice guy who was always motivated, displayed definite leadership skills, and happened to be tall. So, Jacob turned his name into the acronym **T**all **I**ntelligent **M**otivated.

Once, at a professional convention in the United States, I met an exhibitor who was from Norway. He introduced himself, in a heavy Norwegian accent, as **Peter Larsson**. Uncertain if I'd gotten the name right, I asked him to repeat it. He repeated the name and said with a friendly smile: "Peter Larsson. Just think of me as your pal. **Pal—Peter Larsson**."

Meet Pedro Fuentes.

Imagine Pedro puffing on powder. The nickname Puff is based on Pedro's initials: *P* for Pedro, *F* for Fuentes—Puff. Pedro puffing on the powder will remind us of Pedro, and the f in the Puff will remind us of his last name, Fuentes.

Even better, convert a person's name into an acronym in which each word describes the person's traits or characteristics.

Meet Anish Chandak.

Anish works in the physics lab at the Massachusetts Institute of Technology (MIT). **Anish** is **A N**ice **I**ndian **S**cientific **H**ero.

Uncomfortable that we're being politically incorrect here? Great! That's exactly what will engrave the name into your memory. Go ahead and don't be ashamed—use the race bias as a means to remember the face and the name. Don't even be afraid to go off limits with some really insulting associations. (Though I do recommend that you keep this to yourself.) It doesn't indicate your real attitude and level of respect toward the person; it's merely a wacky way to help you remember the name. But if you're really conservative, you can also turn the name Anish into the politically correct: **A** New International Scientific Hero.

LA TECHNIQUE BONAPARTE

The legendary Napoleon Bonaparte was known for his remarkable memory. He set for himself the goal of remembering the names of all his senior officers—a few hundred of them. To achieve this, he developed a unique memory technique. At each introductory meeting, Napoleon used to note the person's name in writing. Then he would look at the name for a few seconds, crumple up the paper, and throw it away. When he looked at the person opposite him again, Napoleon stared at him sharply and imagined the officer's name engraved on his forehead.

Those who use the Napoleon technique have told me that they have refined the method slightly. As soon as they hear a person's name, they imagine how they themselves would engrave the name on that person's forehead. (This could actually be a nice upgrade to world communication, if everyone on earth were to inscribe their name on their forehead. I know, not so practical. What alphabet would be used? And those poor souls with long names, like in Thailand . . .)

Meet Monica Di Stefano.

Imagine engraving the name Monica across her forehead, using a special pen with hot ink as she whimpers in pain from this new tattoo you're giving her. Do it now! Pick up your hand and physically write the name Monica on her actual photo.

In the next chapter, we'll do a short quiz to see which techniques work best for you.

"Well, I have this problem," you may say. "It's kind of hard to meet a new person, carry on a conversation, and at the same time try to make an association between the name and the person. You just can't do that in the middle of talking to someone. What, are we supposed to say, 'Stop! Allow me a minute to visualize your name and associate it with your big nose'? It doesn't work that way."

I've heard this many times before. You don't have to implement a memory technique immediately. This is why God gave us short-term memory. The name-person connection doesn't always come instantaneously. Once you finish a meeting, take a few minutes and then think of a connection.

END A MEETING WITH A STARTING THOUGHT

"Never should a man part from his friend, but with a wise quote, because that's the way he will remember him" it is suggested in the Talmud.

When saying good-bye, say something profound! Instead of tritely saying, "Bye, take care," part in another way—a way that is more unique and attention-grabbing, a way that would be special and distinctive for the individual you've just met. Part with an anecdote, a blessing, or a story, something that will reflect the interaction you just had; something that is relevant only to the two of you and will remind both of you of each other.

Now, let's move on, Ron. Check what you remember, Elmer. And good luck, Chuck.

CHAPTER 20

~~~~~~~~~~~~~~~~~~~~~~~~~~~~~~~~~~~

"EVEN FIVE YEARS LATER . . ."

Determining the Methods That Work Best for You

Paul:	"You look very familiar. Let me guess . . . were you one of my students? Oh, I remember now. You're Dan, right?"
Dan:	"Cut it out, Dad."

I'M GOING TO reintroduce you to the friends we met in the previous chapter. Maybe you'll remember all of them, but most likely you won't. Not to worry. At least, you'll be able to deduce which methods from the range that you've studied are more or less effective for you. Make sure that you have a pen or pencil on hand prior to reviewing the pictures of the people. Okay, let's begin.

Five, ten, or twenty years have elapsed. We're walking along Rue de Rivoli in Paris one pleasant summer evening, when suddenly we see a familiar face walking toward us.

That smile! Those teeth! What was his name . . . do you remember his name?

Write it down: _____

Hardly five minutes have passed, when suddenly a familiar woman approaches us.

What's her name? _____

After we've had a quick espresso and a crêpe Grand Marnier, we return to our chic hotel. There in the lobby, we see another person who left a mark on us.

What's his name? _____

With hardly any time for introductions, the following woman comes through the hotel door:

Her name is _____

We've arranged to meet later at the bar. In the meantime, while walking toward the elevator, the doors open and to our great surprise we see:

His name (first name only—I'll be kind) is_____

And look who's standing next to him!

Hmm . . . what's her first name? _____

Return to the previous chapter and check which names you remembered fully, partially, or not at all.

So, how did you do? Did you remember the names using the nickname method, such as Kim Baker? Or perhaps remembering Monica Di Stefano using the Napoleon technique was more effective. Did the JFK method work for you for recalling Pedro Fuentes and Anish Chandak? I guess the Germans among you remembered Wolfgang Achsman; the Italians, Monica Di Stephano; the Spanish, Pedro Fuentes; and the politically correct, Anish. As we've mentioned, it's only more natural and easier to remember names from a culture to which we belong. However, this does not mean that it's impossible to improve our ability to remember less familiar names.

By the way, do you by any chance remember the tall, muscular doctor . . . the one with the jeep . . . driving on the . . . ?

If you didn't recall any of the names of the people in the previous chapter, or if you remembered only one or two of the names, don't feel that you failed. Success depends on a number of variables: your level of interest, the quality of the associations you make, and other elements.

In order to remember names indefinitely, keep going over your business cards and your contacts, or use the Name Recall software training program I developed with the intention of assisting you with long-term recall of names that are important to you. This software works like a personal trivia game— a simple, enjoyable, and effective way to remember everyone who has crossed your path at various times in your life. You can find more information on this at www.smart-memory.com.

"Memorize the names of thousands of people?" I can hear you say. "I have far more important things to remember! If I try to remember the names of thousands of people I'll probably see only two or three times in my life, this would be at the expense of more important things that I have to remember!"

Let me remind you of the facts we discussed at the beginning of this book.

1. Throughout our entire lifetime, we don't exploit even 10 percent of our memory's capacity. Every single day, we remember hundreds, even thousands of information units; every thought, idea, word, sound, item, and name is absorbed and preserved in our memory. The bottom line is that the thousands of names that you would want to remember won't even *scratch* the memory volume available in your head!

2. The more memory "uploaded" into our brain, the more our mind will improve, working more efficiently; it can even reduce the chances of memory problems in old age.

Try using these methods, and one day when you come across a past acquaintance on the street, at the mall, or in the middle of the Amazon, you will immediately remember that person's name and make a terrific impression.

~~~~~~~~~~~~~~~~~~~~~~~~~~~~~~~~~~

CHAPTER 21

THE PLAYING CARDS STUNT

NOW FOR SOME extra credit. Ask a friend to take a deck of cards and shuffle it well. When he's done, take the deck and look at the cards, one after the other. You'll be able to repeat the order of the cards from beginning to end, and from end to beginning. Plus, you'll be able to repeat the order of the cards starting at any random point in the middle of the deck!

As you probably know, the cards are divided into four categories: spades, hearts, clubs, and diamonds. Let's give each shape a letter:

Spades: S
Hearts: R
Clubs: C
Diamonds: D

The idea is to take any card you see and convert it into a word. This word will contain the letter that was given to the category and the letter that represents the number of the card (according to the conversion table you learned in Chapter 11). First the shape, then the card's number. For instance, if you are shown the four of clubs, you may convert it in the following way: clubs will be C and the 4 will be R. Now we can see that the four of clubs is *car*.

What word can be derived from the eight of diamonds'? Diamonds is D and the 8 is V. We can create a new word: *dove*.

What is the ace of hearts? According to the rules of playing cards, the ace is 1. So hearts becomes R and the ace (1) becomes T. The two combined are *rat*.

What can we do about the jack, queen, and king? The jack is represented by J, SH, or soft G. Let's say you have the jack of hearts. Hearts is R, the jack is SH: *rash*. The queen can be K, hard C, or hard G. For example, with the queen of clubs, clubs is C, the queen is K—*cake*. The king . . . ah, the king is naked. This means no letter will represent it. What shock, what embarrassment! The king cards will be treated as the category only. For example, when you see a king of diamonds, you will only need to remember the word *diamond*.

The method of remembering an entire deck of cards is easy. Each card is converted into a word. Then a chain of associations has to be created, as we've learned before.

Let's assume our deck contains the following cards: two of diamonds, eight of hearts, jack of clubs, ace of spades, and king of hearts. We'll quickly convert the cards into words:

Two of diamonds—D, N—*den*.
Eight of hearts—R, F—*roof*.
Jack of clubs—C, G—*cage*.
Ace of spades—S, T—*seat*.
King of hearts—*heart*.

These five meaningless cards are easily turned into five words: *den*, *roof*, *cage*, *seat*, and *heart*. Let's now connect them in an associative story or chain.

Imagine you're sitting in the den, when suddenly the roof caves in. You run into a secure cage and sit on the comfortable seat inside it. Now you really feel your heart beating . . .

Ready to convert the words back into the order of the cards? *Den* turns into the two of diamonds, *roof* becomes the eight of hearts, *cage* is now the jack of clubs, *seat* turns into the ace of spades, and *heart* is the king of hearts.

It's very important that you memorize the method of converting cards into words *prior* to performing card stunts around the world.

CHAPTER 22

THE LONG NUMBER STUNT

THIS IS ONE of my favorites. Remembering a list that consists of one hundred items seems to be an impossible mission. If such is the case, then remembering a number made up of a hundred digits, after hearing it only once, must seem to indicate some sort of a mental disturbance.

As I've mentioned, I perform this stunt in my lectures (check them out on YouTube or my website, www.erankatz .com). I ask people in the audience to call out digits in the range of 0 to 9. I write these digits on a board, until I reach a number made of thirty to forty digits. It looks like this:

3248676930285765242313956593038475665689

Once I finish writing the number, I repeat it from beginning to end and from end to beginning.

I know what's behind the amazed expressions on the audience's faces. "He must be some sort of idiot savant," they think. "No one is able to perform such a stunt." I "apologize" and declare that I am no genius and that I do not possess a phenomenal memory. All I have is a simple method that I've mastered.

By the way, it's with this stunt that I made it into *The Guinness Book of Records*. After attorney Ilan Shemer read me a five-hundred-digit number, a hundred digits at a time—I repeated those digits, with just four mistakes. And now let me teach you how to remember a long number. We'll begin by memorizing a twenty-digit number.

Pay attention to the following: 42215172910793504327. (By the way, this is the number which appeared in Quiz #3 in Chapter 3.)

You probably realize by now how this is done. The way to remember a long number is to turn the digits into letters. We will convert each pair of digits into a word (picture) with a visual meaning. By doing so, we won't need to try to remember twenty meaningless digits. Instead, we will only need to remember ten words—more correctly, ten pictures.

As a reminder, you were already able to easily remember a list of ten items at the beginning of this book!

First, we'll break the number up into pairs: 42, 21, 51, 72, 91, 07, 93, 50, 43, 27.

Then we'll turn each pair of digits into a word: 42 = *rain*, 21 = *net*, 51 = *lead*, 72 = *can*, 91 = *bed*, 07 = *sack*, 93 = *bum*, 50 = *lace*, 43 = *room*, 27 = *neck*.

The final step is to weave associations between the words.

You are standing in the *rain*. You feel it pouring over you, so you search for something to cover yourself with. You pick up a *net* and wrap it over your head (yes, not too bright an idea—it won't really stop you from getting wet). But then you find a *lead* apron (the kind you wear when having an X-ray taken) and pull that over your head. Now a new problem arises—this lead sheet is quite heavy. So you just throw it into the large garbage *can* near where you are standing. Hey! Look! Someone threw away a *bed,* and it is just standing there next to the can! On the bed there is a large *sack.* Next to the sack lies its legal owner—a *bum,* gripping it tightly. You try to disconnect the bum from the sack, but you see it's tied to him by a string of *lace* (wow, that lace is strong). So you give up trying to untangle the lace. You look at the other side of it and see that it is actually coming out of an open *room* to your left, which you obviously failed to notice before. You crane your *neck* to see what's inside the room, and hurt your neck while doing so . . .

Now, let's check what we remember.

Our story begins when we are standing in the rain. To what digits can we convert *rain*? 42. What do we want to do? Cover ourselves with the net. What does *net* turn into? 21. This net isn't helpful, but luckily there is a lead apron next to us. *Lead* = 51. The lead is too heavy, so we toss it into the large can. *Can* = 72.

What's next to the can? A bed someone threw away. *Bed* is 91. On the bed lies a large sack. We will convert *sack* into 07. What's lying next to this sack? A bum—*bum* is 93. How are the two tied? With lace . . . and *lace* is 50. This lace leads to a room. What's our *room*? Correct, it's 43. To peek in, you stretch out your neck—and *neck* is 27.

What happens if you are asked to repeat this number from end to beginning? Just go over your story from end to beginning, like a movie played backward: your neck hurts, meaning 27. But pay attention! You have to take each pair of digits and switch their order. This now means that you have to announce the 7 first, because 7 is the last digit of the long number. Only after it is the 2 placed, because 2 is the next to last digit. If we keep thinking about our story in reverse, we are peeking into a room. *Room* is 43. We will announce the 3 first . . . 327. Now comes the 4 . . . 4327. Why were we looking inside the room? This is because a string of lace came out of it. *Lace* is 50. But this 50 will be announced backward— first the 0 . . . 04327. Following is 5 . . . 504327. Continue in the same fashion until you reach the rain. Finally, *rain* will be converted into 42. Announce 2. And now . . . 4.

Receive a round of enthusiastic applause and bow graciously. You've done it!

CHAPTER 23

~~~~~~~~~~~~~~~~~~~~~~~~~

SO WHERE *DID* NOAH PARK THE ARK?

The Importance of a Blessed Memory

IN GENESIS 6:14-17 it's clearly indicated: "And when Noah finished his shopping at the Mesopotamian Mall, he circled the parking lot and couldn't find the ark. The livestock, who came in pairs, were exhausted from the long day, especially the male animals, who had to carry the shopping bags . . . Finally, the wise dove flapped her wings and whispered in Noah's ear: 'Mount Ararat, Noah! Area B14—between the *Mayflower* and the *Bismarck*.'"

Actually, theologians are not clear on the ark's final parking spot. Mount Ararat, the rumored location, sits at the border of Iran and Russia and is too high for a boat to land. Based on geographical logic, it's likely that the ark rested at the base of the mountain, where the Tigris and Euphrates rivers flow.

In truth, Noah didn't really need the ark after the flood was over, so he didn't need to remember where he parked it. The point being, it's not necessary to remember everything.

The advantage of having a trained memory is that we're able to remember anything we *choose* to remember. It would be senseless to memorize—word for word—a daily newspaper, for example.

You may theorize that many executives have secretaries to help them remember important meetings. But do you believe that the executives would have reached their impressive achievements if they didn't have a good memory themselves? And how long do you think a secretary would be employed if she didn't have a good memory?

It's crucial for a court litigator to remember the facts in his questioning. If he needs to look at his notes while doing so, it wouldn't look very professional. A surgeon must know everything before and during an operation. She can't refer to her *Heart Transplant for Dummies* book every few minutes.

Writing this book has been a personal mission for me. I really, truly believe that people with a better memory can create a better society.

He who remembers the names of people is a person who loves mankind. Such a person takes an interest in others and cares about them. If students knew that they could trust their memory and recall a tremendous amount of knowledge, many negative phenomena could be avoided, like cheating on exams and cutthroat classroom competition.

What happens to someone who's in a hurry to leave the house and can't find his car keys? It begins with "I don't get it! I just had them in my hand." It continues fifteen minutes later with "If I don't find these keys, I'm going to kill somebody." When this person finally gets into his car, he is extremely agitated.

He's so upset at being fifteen minutes late that he might, God forbid, even get into an accident.

By now, I do believe that you're aware of the importance of a good memory. Most of you would like to have one. The proof lies in your hands right now. You have just finished reading a book about it.

Now you face a choice. You can close this book, place it on your bookshelf, and go on with your life as if you've never read it. Or you can implement some of the methods you have learned.

If you decide to try some of the techniques, do so gradually, and treat the process as a fun game. Begin with simple matters—with the things that were easier for you to do while reading this book. Step by step, you'll find that implementing these techniques becomes instinctive. This will tremendously improve your memory and the quality of your life.

Ten years ago, I walked into an office. On the wall I saw a sign with the following written on it that later became a motto in my life: "Don't let the person inside you interfere with the person that you can be."

Try to use these methods. Try every new thing you learn!

And know that you are capable of remembering anything you want to remember.

ACKNOWLEDGMENTS

I WOULD LIKE to thank some precious friends and family members who contributed to the birth of this book: My agent, Scott Hoffman, who never gave up until we hit a home run. Mary Choteborsky, my editor, the jewel of the Crown, for her vote of confidence and vision. Julie Rothschild Levi for her critic's eye, perfectionism, and friendship. Steve Safran and Cheli Rozenbach for their professional contributions. My loving girls: Gali, Tamari, Guli, and that cat we have (forgot its name . . .). Dr. Shelly Katz, my mother, who introduced me to the world of brain skills.

Idan, Tal, Tom, Bar, Shiri, Rafi Givon, and Ellen Carmel. Eran Bar-Tal, Lenny Ravich, Alon Friedman, Isaac Lavi, Guy and Sarit Olamy, Mehmet Ogutcu, Spiros Diamantis, Maya Crevecoeur, and Chieko Maruyama.

But most of all, you, for reading this book. We may have never met, but you are a part of me now.

INDEX

abbreviations, organizing using,
65–66
absorbing, effective, attention
and, 36–37
academic success. *See* school
success
acronyms
parallel, 68–71
reverse, 66–68, 206–7
acrostics, organizing using,
66–67
age as excuse for failing to
remember, 8–9
appearances, remembering,
215–23
Aryeh, Yehuda, 82
"association disorder," 42
associations, 41–53
to connect key words,
169–70
for foreign language
learning, 199–202
imagination and, 43–47

between names and
appearances, 216–18
reconstructing associative
stories and, 174–77
remembering to diet and,
101–2
remembering to perform a
task or action and,
96–98
rules for creating, 52–53
sense sharing and, 47–53
word-resemblance method
for, 171–72
attention
distributing correctly,
39–40
effective absorbing and,
36–37
elevating level of, 37–38
during lectures, 156–57
as most important element
of memory, 40
attitude, 54–62

Index